MW01147136

Who
Wins
and Why

Fifty Keys to Victory in Sports, Business, and the Game of Life

Stephen Weigert, M.S.
Psychotherapist, Athlete, Actor and Race Car Driver

Who Wins and Why:
Fifty Keys to Victory in Sports, Business, and the Game of Life

Stephen Weigert, M.S.
Psychotherapist, athlete, actor, and race car driver

ISBN: 978-1-98352-877-4

Contents

INTRODUCTION

Do you dream of living in a prestigious community, traveling to exotic locations, wearing designer clothes, and driving a Mercedes, Porsche, Bentley, or Rolls Royce?

Would you like to be able to achieve this?

I did it. So can you.

What does it require? The time it will take you to read two short books.

This book, "Who Wins and Why" is the first of the pair, and it's already at your fingertips. A copy of the second book can be found both online and in new and used bookstores.

You have taken the time to read this introduction to "Who Wins and Why," because you've come to the conclusion that you want to change your life. You want to win. It doesn't matter what it is that prompted this realization. Neither your age, your gender, or your marital status factor into your decision. This is a personal choice. You've simply decided that now is the perfect time to take charge of your life and chart a course for success. Your subconscious has obviously been paying attention. Your subconscious is usually right.

Shall I tell you more?

I came from a middle-class background with parents who were well-educated but never ostentatious or materialistic. They were surprised, I think, by my early fascination with the finer things in life, but they never discouraged me. I was a youngster who preferred Saks Fifth Avenue clothing—albeit from the clearance/seconds/discontinued racks, as I could afford those items from my paper route and odd job earnings.

As a kid, I often carried with me a well-worn copy of F. Scott Fitzgerald's book, "The Great Gatsby." I found myself fascinated by phrases and scenes which memorialized wonderful adventures and the perks of great wealth. Admittedly, my childhood "dreams" were adventures initially beyond my reach— auto racing, climbing to a mountain summit (I climbed local water towers for practice), surfing in the Pacific—and in the similarly distant material rewards, the fine furnishings and luxurious dwellings usually reserved for the truly affluent.

Regardless, those dreams managed to stay with me throughout high school and then college, where I found myself intrigued by the study of psychology.

As a young adult, I had visualized myself with an impressive waterfront home, a fast boat, a black Bentley, and a white Rolls-Royce in the driveway. As unlikely as all that seemed at the time to some of those around me, the adventures I'd aspired to and those things I'd pictured, all eventually came to be in my life.

As a professional counselor, psychotherapist, and life coach for over forty years, my focus has been on helping people. I experienced the unparalleled exhilaration of seeing people from all walks of life, all ages, and all financial situations, transform themselves in some way for the better. All of those I worked with gained something positive, and some eventually succeeded far beyond their wildest expectations.

While my focus was mainly on helping others to get ahead, the concepts I taught carried over profoundly into my own aspirations and visions of an exciting and affluent lifestyle.

What I realized early on was that the best approach in helping others wasn't so much about the "problem" as it was about the success that awaited them if they could be shown the path, including the belief systems, proven strategies, and essential action steps to get there. In that sense, the concepts which I've outlined in this book are universal and are representative of what I've shared with each of the thousands of people who came to me for guidance over the years.

The principles of "deliberate practice" apply not only to athletes but also to the method in which any individual achieves correctly performed skills, and then mentally "programs" these skills to become automatic when needed.

While I was coaching others I added any newly discovered strategies, my "Aha!" moments, to the kaleidoscope of my own dreams and aspirations. As a helping professional, I also made it a point to actually "test" the performance "formulas" myself, before advocating them to others.

Success and winning are actually less about talent and more about identifying and acting upon a small number of essential beliefs and critical steps necessary for a victory. If you can picture yourself achieving something (visualizing it in detail), there's a great chance you can actually do it.

The *will to win* can be objectively defined and identified. It's applying your ability to do everything that is necessary to achieve your goals in life, sports, or any endeavor you care to undertake. Others may think it can't be done, but your laser-sharp focus, desire, preparation, and your expectation of a win prevail. These components of the *will to win* can be learned and are accelerated by adherence to principles of integrity.

What can legitimately be considered a *win* arises from a foundation of personal and professional integrity, i.e., principles and a code of conduct based on consistent truthfulness, and a respect for others.

There's a habit which, if integrated into everyday thinking, brings one *much closer to winning*. It's the ability to *PAY ATTENTION*. When you think about it, it's a *lack* of attention, whether in business, sports, or in life, that is the direct cause of most of our mistakes, "accidents," interpersonal problems, or financial miscues.

A similarly important habit toward winning, particularly in personal and business matters, is one's comfort level with saying "No." Most of us have difficulty saying and meaning it. That reluctance leads us into commitments that we don't have time for or don't wish to do. It can place us in uncomfortable, often unproductive situations with those around us, and often leads to ineffective negotiation.

"Learning isn't so important, it's what kind of [person] you make out of yourself while you're learning that counts," said Dale Carnegie, author of the iconic "How To Win Friends And Influence People." That's the second book you'll want to read. It's been ranked by the Library of Congress as the 7th most influential book in American history.

Carnegie maintained that success could be found by charm, appreciation, and personality. He also explained how to use the egotistical tendencies of other people to one's advantage. He too made it a point to actually "test" each of his performance "formulas" himself, before advocating them to others.

Experience is a great teacher, yet in preparing to win, it's critically important that one not learn everything by trial and error. It simply takes too long. It's better to learn from another's experiences and insight. Someone else has already spent the time and paid the price of failed options until a winning strategy emerged. You don't need to reinvent the wheel.

Observe, study, and learn.

#1. ON GAINING A PSYCHOLOGICAL ADVANTAGE

To win you'll need a psychological advantage over your opponent.

Most professional athletes will agree that winning is at least 50 percent mental. It comes from confidence in knowing that you've o*ver-prepared* and the calmness that follows. Stress enters our minds mainly from what we know we should have done but didn't do. The key question is "Who do you think you are?" All your behavior and all of your accomplishments or set-backs are shaped by who you think you are—your self-perception. Every individual tends to receive what he or she expects in the long run—often programmed at an unconscious level at an early age.

In the boxing film, "Creed," aging Rocky Balboa (Sylvester Stallone) tells the young fighter, Creed, "This guy here. That's the toughest opponent you're ever going to face," as Creed looks in a mirror. Rocky adds, "I think that's true in the ring and I think that's true in life." To a great extent, one loses not because of a lack of ability, but instead from a subtle weakness in their self-image—a mental *roadblock*, so to speak.

Physician/author, Maxwell Maltz, M.D., maintained a premise that "New roles require new self-images." One of the most important mental attributes we can develop as we grow up is *self-discipline.* It's about having a plan and an unbreakable code or promise to ourselves in following the steps to achieve the plan's objective.

Surprisingly, in academic success, self-discipline is twice as accurate as IQ in predicting a student's grade point average. But it's not just in academics or in the game. Having a supposedly high IQ doesn't assure that you'll make quality decisions. And what difference does it really make if it's something we can't *change*? Winners focus precisely on what can be changed and improved. Self-discipline can be acquired and consistently applied. It keeps one fully on course to *win*.

A key indicator of self-discipline is revealed in how you handle criticism or rejection. A calm and objective response says more about your character than a juvenile attack on your critic.

ACTION STEP: Take time to assess your *self-concept.* Be brutally honest in looking at your level of confidence, attitude toward preparation, your typical self-talk, and your self-discipline.

#2. ON LETTING GO

Once they're in a game, winners have "let go" of *having* to win.

While enthusiasm and concentrated effort are essential parts of preparation, an intentional effort on winning (*trying* intensely to win) is actually a major deterrent to success. Winners have learned that a focused relaxation of effort allows a natural flow of peak performance. At critical moments, a winner simply relies upon the high quality techniques he or she has practiced without mentally entering into the tension or pressure present on the court or field. A winning football kicker isn't thinking about a negative outcome ("I *can't miss* this crucial field goal!") but instead has a clear and simple image of each of the times he's *made it* in the past.

Victor Frankl, Holocaust survivor and author, called this important concept "paradoxical intention" and explained that it applies particularly to winning and to happiness. "The more we aim at it, the more we miss our aim."

ACTION STEP: In your game—any game or challenge—relax your need to win and concentrate instead on consistency in your performance and visualizing each step at your highest level of skill.

#3. ON OBSERVATION

You win by careful *observation.*

Model the specific actions and strategies of those who are already champions.

Learning as much as you can about how the "heroes" in your sport or industry made it happen is an essential foundation for your own success. If it worked for them it can work for you. Identify in detail what your hero did along the way, including any set-backs they had to overcome. Then your performance from that mental template is as if you *are* that champion playing.

Read the biographies and autobiographies of those you admire. Watch documentaries that profile their lives and accomplishments. Become *one* with them as you observe their journeys and sense their emotions along the way.

ACTION STEP: Pick several models or mentors who've demonstrated the skills and accomplishments you hope to gain. Mirror your heroes! If you can't meet them, *learn* about them.

#4. ON THE DETAILS

It's in the *details*—it all counts.

In a winning lifestyle, each action and decision you make, the minor as well as the significant stuff, sets your path. A sign in the U.S. Olympic Training Centre reads: "Not every four years—EVERY DAY!" I'm a firm believer in the concept that *"It's all in the details."* One small slip or oversight, whether on the court, field, racetrack, or in business can derail an otherwise smooth path to victory.

A remarkable and rarely recognized fact about success and winning has been revealed over time in analysis of athletes going for the gold in Olympic competition. It's true outside of sports in many business and personal endeavors as well. The difference in times or scores from winners to the other competitors is often no more than 3 percent! From my auto racing days, I recall that several years ago for the Indy 500 race, the qualifying lap times for the race's starting order varied by just one second, total, from the pole position (#1) to last place (#33).

In business, the most successful organizations *sweat the small stuff*—they get compulsive about the details. On the athletic field and in every aspect of your personal life, PAY ATTENTION! It pays off. Lack of attention, not lack of skill, explains most of the miscues in athletics and in the professional and private challenges

16

that really matter—including those rare but sometimes fatal mistakes made by experienced drivers and pilots.

ACTION STEP: Practice paying attention to details. DO sweat the small stuff!

#5. ON SPEAKING YOUR GAME

How you speak your game is as important as how you play it.

It's both *what you say to others* and your *self-talk.* There is tremendous power in your words, the linguistic elements—the "charge," positive or negative, of each word. You will be judged by what you say to others before, during, and after a game (or audition, interview, negotiation, etc.)—and you can't take it back. And the charge (negative or positive) of the words you've selected and told yourself quickly gets programmed into your subconscious.

Our words, spoken or written, shape who we become. Your image and your actions reflect your worth and your concern for the well-being of others. When you're winning, some will admire you and some will resent your success. To win in the long run, you need the continuing support, loyalty, and admiration of others. Baseball manager Tommy Lasorda commented, "Never tell your troubles to your friends. Eighty percent of them don't care, and the other twenty percent are glad." There's nothing accomplished in whining. If you're not happy about a situation, just *do something* about it.

Everyone should have, readily available, a great "story" about what you do, how you got where you are, what's important to you, and how you see your future. It should be short, concise, yet inviting and somewhat intriguing. Your brief story will define the first impression you make on others. If you wish to convince others of *anything*, the format of a story is often your best tool.

ACTION STEP: Prepare a brief but *great* story of who you are, what's important to you, and how you see your future. Look for an opportunity to use it.

#6. BEING ABLE TO DO ANYTHING

Anyone can learn to do anything.

It's really as simple as that. With technology, more than at any other time in history, it's possible for us to quickly learn the basics about any sport, recreational activity, business opportunity, exercise, therapy—anything! A few years ago, I signed up for equestrian polo lessons without ever having ridden a horse. Before the training, I learned how to ride by watching You Tube videos. On the polo field, no one ever suspected my unconventional entry into the sport. The experienced horse I was assigned to seemed to know exactly what to do without much guidance from me. I scored the first goal!

It's important to dispel the myth that outstanding athletes, entertainers, business leaders, and other accomplished professionals were *born* with more talent than the rest of us. Instead, it's about *learning* to win.

Jeff Rosenthal, co-founder of the Summit Series of inspirational events for highly successful young entrepreneurs and professionals. told a Town and Country magazine reporter, "We're in the age of the polymath (a person of encyclopedic learning). Never before have more people had more information about various different things at the same time, and the parallel innovation and collaboration of those things reinforce one another and really create the near future." We can access online a fact or trivial statistic instantly and can be inspired by an expert on nearly any topic by viewing a brief TED talk.

Of course, the learning and retention of new knowledge or a new skill takes time.

Future Hall of Fame quarterback Peyton Manning retired in early 2016 after his eighteen-year career with two Super Bowl victories and five MVP awards. He reflected, "There were other players that were more talented than me but there was no one who could out-prepare me."

The *preparation* Manning spoke of is essentially learning something by *experiencing.* Sensing it. Feeling it. Becoming one with it. Experiencing a new skill area or challenge at its strongest instructional level requires doing that and that alone. What this means is that any distracting thoughts, fears, or doubts are counter-productive.

Manning's focus on preparation actually has significance in its surprising relationship to positive mental attitude, which alone, as I noted earlier, isn't a determinant of success. What the relationship means, according to well-known motivational author Robert Ringer, is that positive mental attitude is not a *cause* of success but instead a *result* of being prepared. Its value, particularly, is as a tool for maintaining confidence in the face of a series of consecutive failures.

In the 1960s at the peak of his young career as a counter-culture singer and musician, Guru Singh, born Gerry Pond, left his promising path for a spiritual journey into higher consciousness in the remote mountains of

Mexico. In his recent book, *Buried Treasure: The Journey from Where You Are to Who You Are,* he relates climbing a high mountain with two 80-year-old companions who reached the summit far ahead of him, a fit 20-year-old at the time. The young Pond, years before his "rebirth" as Guru Singh, asked the elders their secret. They replied, simply, "The only difference is that when we climb the mountain, our bodies and minds and emotions are only climbing the mountain and nothing else." A hidden key from some wise old men.

Just in the past few years, real-time human brain imaging and research have advanced to a point where a subject's processing of information and sensory data can be graphically pin-pointed within the brain. This ground-breaking science identifies the most effective learning techniques and can allow *anyone* to achieve peak performance in sports, business, academic, and personal pursuits. It's exciting!

Regarding the way our brain *actually* processes new information compared to what we've been led to believe in education and through self-help materials and programs, the next sentence will likely surprise and shock you. Most of what we're taught conventionally and just about all of what's presented to us in self-help programs, books, lectures, and CD's *simply doesn't work!*

With as much as we see, hear, and read every day, our brain dismisses most of it within a few minutes unless we've attached significance to the information and have begun to process it into our subconscious. Making a permanent change in our thinking and behavior doesn't happen instantly. It involves consciously attaching importance to the idea, acting on and *experiencing* it, and sustaining the idea for a period of at least twenty-one to thirty days or so. Only then is the new information and action fully programmed into our subconscious.

ACTION STEP: Pick some activity far from your regular interests and jump into it!

#7. ON BEING A STUDENT

You must first be a student before you can become a master.

This book provides validation and expansion of winning concepts and explores a "library," so to speak, of thought-provoking insights into how, exactly, one *wins*— the concepts that most of us simply haven't been taught. Alone, the good intentions of experienced teachers and coaches aren't enough. John Wooden, the masterful UCLA basketball coach, often said, "It's what you learn after you know it all that really counts."

More than anything else, what separates winners from losers is that winners *take action.* Just as Peyton Manning did consistently, they simply do what needs to be done. There's a universal truth, "How you do anything is how you do everything." Often overlooked, the habits of our daily thinking and tasks reveal, indeed, how we will handle the important challenges and goals in our lives.

As to my own background, let me explain that I'm a *collector.* Since childhood, I've collected the great ideas and strategies of others. In that 1925 classic book, *The Great Gatsby,* which I carried around In my boyhood, this fictional Jay Gatsby kept a written schedule of his daily planning in the back open pages of *his* favorite book, *Hopalong Cassidy*: "Rise from bed, 6 am; exercise, 6:15-6:30 am; study electricity, etc., 7:15-8:15 am; ...practice elocution, poise, and how to attain it, 5:00 pm-6:00 pm," and so on. Among "General Resolves," young Gatsby included "read one improving book or magazine per week." And so I did. For me, one book or magazine a week was never enough and still isn't. *The Great Gatsby*, although fiction, provided me with a template and strategies toward a colorful lifestyle and self-directed accomplishments. Draw inspiration from the productive habits and accomplishments of others!

As I noted earlier, I've outlined the "best of the best" observations and strategies I've absorbed from others and also what I've learned first-hand over the years as they apply to winning and success. To believe it, I had to live it . What did I learn? Essentially, that winners are *made*, not born.

ACTION STEP: Write an inventory of what you feel you'll need to learn—the specific skills—to achieve your chosen level of success.

#8. ON SHOWING UP

Success comes from *showing up* and from *taking action.*
While Woody Allen says, "Eighty percent of success is *showing up*," I'd add that the remaining 20 percent comes invariably from taking action, often *any* action, to gain momentum toward your goal. The way our brains work, taking action, particularly a bold action, pushes our cognitive functioning into high gear. It expands our mental capacity to perform, and it gives us *power* and accelerated stamina

For many of us, success comes from specific actions formed by a well-disciplined and demanding program of training from an early age. For others, success and winning, whether in sports, performing, or in business, does come rather quickly, often from being at the right place at the right time.

Tennis icon Andre Agassi shares in his autobiography, *Open*, that his father, Mike, while coaching young Andre, told him that if he hit 2500 balls each day, he'd hit 17,500 balls each week, and at the end of one year he'd have hit nearly one million balls.

"Numbers don't lie. A child who hits one million balls each year will be unbeatable," Mike insisted. Under relentless pressure from his father, Andre hit that million balls. And during his twenty-year tennis career, he was often ranked number one in the world.

As a thirteen-year-old, Lance Armstrong joined his Plano, Texas swim club. He trained from 5:30 am to 7 am, swimming four miles daily, plus riding his bike 10 miles each day between his home, the swim club, and school. Lance soon added running six miles each day after school. At age fourteen, he entered a junior triathalon and won. As a high school senior, Lance completed the Junior World Championship bike races in Moscow and then joined the U.S. National Cycling Team.

Hall of Fame baseball player, Ted Williams, took 1000 swings a day, probably 900 swings more than anyone else. That's why hitting came easy for him.

However, as my own sport of auto racing reveals, the way to the top sometimes takes months instead of years. In 2006, nineteen-year-old Marco Andretti, likely inheriting some talent and encouragement from his racing ancestors, nearly won the very *first* Indy 500 race in which he competed, achieving second place in one of the closest finishes in Indy history.

In Europe in 2010, twenty-three-year-old German, Sebastian Vettel, won the Formula 1 championship, the highest international level of racing. In that same series , talented sixteen-year-old Dutch driver Max Verstappan became the youngest F1 driver ever, not yet legally old enough to get his regular Dutch driver's license! In 2016, at age eighteen, he became the youngest driver ever to *win* an F1 race.

For most of us, though, winning isn't that simple. There's something we miss and the actions we take are unproductive. Author Dan Ariely in his 2008 book, *Predictably Irrational,* describes how expectations, emotions, social norms, and other invisible, seemingly illogical forces skew our ability to win. Ariely demonstrates how we not only make astonishingly simple mistakes every day, but how we make the same *types* of mistakes repeatedly.

Ariely's premise is essentially that when it comes to making decisions in our lives, we think we're making smart, rational choices—but we often fail to understand the profound effects of our emotions on what we want, and we make *illogical* choices. Recognizing this tendency, I think, brings us closer to making logical, practical decisions and taking the most productive *action* in sports, in business, and in the game of life.

Author Robin Sharma, in his book *The Greatness Guide*, reminds us "The smallest of actions is always better than the noblest of intentions." I'd add that most of what we accomplish results from *momentum.* Our first action starts the process that gains momentum and builds strength as the task moves along.

ACTION STEP: Estimate and chart how much time daily or weekly you expect you'll need to put in to bring your present skills and performance to a *winning* level.

#9. ON MATCHING YOUR ACTION TO YOUR GOAL

Once we understand how to make highest level choices, our *action* has to fit our *goal*.

By the time I started auto racing in 1983, I'd observed many new drivers over my decades as a spectator. It seemed clear to me over time that most novice drivers made similarly predictable and costly mistakes. For that reason, after a year or so, only a few of the aspiring young drivers remained in competition. Their motorsports dream had somehow faded and dematerialized along the way.

Before I began my racing career I applied what I'd observed, and I narrowed my focus down to three essential criteria which I had identified as necessary for my success.

I'd noted, for example, that most novice drivers brought to the required SCCA Driving School events race cars that they had purchased as fairly worn-out, ill-prepared vehicles.

A novice driver is required to complete a fairly high number of on-track hours and novice race sessions, all within the season in which they're attempting to earn a racing license. If those hours and sessions aren't completed, the novice essentially has to start all the hours and sessions over during the next season if he or she still wants to work toward a racing license.

Accordingly, the first key criterion I set for myself was that I'd start in a *new* rather than used race car so that I could concentrate on the driving without the setbacks from mechanical failures. That cost more, of course, so I had to save for several years to purchase a new Volkswagen GTI and have it professionally set-up as a race car. The owners of the dealership I selected, father and son, raced Volkswagens on the pro circuit and quite capably set up my car to be competitive. It didn't make sense to learn by trial and error. That first criterion--having a new, fully dependable race car--served me well, and I completed the novice race training on schedule.

My second criterion, by observation, was that as a rookie driver in races, I *had* to keep up my speed with the rest of the cars in the field. A slow driver on the race course presents a hazard to the faster competitors. As a newcomer to racing, this often took me out of my comfort-zone but it advanced my learning curve as well. I forced myself to closely follow the faster competitors. Had I consistently fallen behind the others, my deficiency would have been obvious to race officials and I'd have been determined "not ready" for safe competition.

My third criterion as a new race driver was that besides maintaining adequate, consistent speed, I simply could not get in the way of the faster drivers, many of them already at the pro level, when they were passing/lapping me on the track. Rookie drivers often fail to see or be aware of a faster car behind them and create close-calls or crashes when they obstruct or cut off the faster car. The quickest path to end your race days are complaints from veteran drivers that you "don't belong on the track."

Accordingly, I kept an eye on my mirrors and acknowledged faster drivers as they approached—a simple point of my orange-gloved finger though the small window opening—so that they knew I saw them and they could pass on that side. Many times, the veteran racers thanked me for being observant. Once I'd been passed, I often forced myself to get out of my comfort-zone and literally follow that faster driver as closely as I could, using their "line" around the track, their braking and turn-in points— mirroring the faster competitor. Of course I, too, got *faster.*

My three on-track criteria continued to serve me well over the seventeen seasons I raced—without any crashes or even any damage, and I finished every race! An unusual record, and luck played a part in it, I'm sure. While most of my Regional U.S. and National/Pro race events were in sports cars, I added various on-track sessions over the years in NASCAR, IndyCar, and Mercedes AMG Challenge events.

I'll share that my personally-funded budget for racing over the years was well below that of most competitors and their teams. My team's tools and spares at the track were in cardboard boxes. Without paddock tents, we parked our race cars under a tree, if possible, for shade. And without a motor home, I stood in line with the spectators at the portable toilets to change in and out of my race suit. There's more than one way to enter and participate in an upper level sport. And sometimes we *won*!

Overall, I had learned to race *smart,* efficiently, and within budget. Change the venue from a race track to a new business or starting a career and the strategies work just as well.

ACTION STEP: Whether in your sport, business, or your path as an entertainer, take the time to prioritize among the many activities or tasks. Identify your top three as the key guides in your decisions and strategies.

#10. ON YOUR UNLIMITED POTENTIAL

We start life with *unlimited potential.*

In his book *How to Succeed in Sport and Life*, Dan Millman reminds us that we all begin life as master athletes with nearly unlimited potential. But through limiting beliefs, emotional conflicts, and physical tensions, Millman explains, we lose touch with many of our childhood skills.

Aldous Huxley stated: "In all activities of life, the secret of efficiency lies in an ability to combine two seemingly incompatible states: a state of maximum activity and a state of maximum relaxation." Adding to this insight, authors Janet and Chris Atwood in *The Passion Test: The Effortless Path to Discovering Your Life Purpose* maintain that the most profound secret of life is essentially that one creates whatever he or she chooses to have in their life by Intention, Attention, and No-Tension.

What this means, simply, is that to "win," one has clarified in detail—precisely—their *intention*; has sharply focused their *attention* on the task and the essential steps to accomplish it; and has learned that an inner state of calm (*no-tension*) allows them to move forward easily and comfortably to a winning result. Interestingly, along this path the intention is to perform the necessary steps flawlessly while simply remaining *unattached* to the outcome.

Even in unconventional pursuits, winning is the result of carefully refined traits and strategies. An accomplished Marine sniper, Corporal Steve Krueger, describes what makes a good military sniper: "Very self-reliant, a lot of confidence, but easy-going. A lot of common sense too."

See if you can regain the relaxed, creative learning style you had as a child. You tried something new in various ways until it worked. You couldn't fail!

ACTION STEP: Renew and apply the best elements of your childhood's carefree attitude within your present learning and in your challenges and struggles.

#11. ON THE LESSONS FROM HISTORY

History reveals a lot about winning.

In the 1976 U.S. presidential election, low-profile Georgia peanut farmer and one-term Governor, Jimmy Carter, won over incumbent and generally well-regarded President, Gerald Ford.

TV actress Susan Lucci was unsuccessfully nominated for eighteen years for an "Outstanding Lead Actress" Emmy for her highly popular role in the soap opera, *All My Children*, until finally getting the award in 1999.

In 1998, Jesse Ventura, former pro wrestler and considered by political insiders to "not have a chance," won the Minnesota Governor's election over two popular, experienced, and well-qualified candidates.

In the 2014 French Open international tennis tournament, sisters Venus and Serena Williams, with multiple World #1 rankings and usually considered "unbeatable," both lost to newcomers (nineteen and twenty years old) in the early Second Round.

Legendary golfer Tiger Woods was ranked World #1 for 281 consecutive weeks, from June, 2005 through October, 2010, and then was winless in tournaments for the next 107 weeks until December, 2011, having dropped to a ranking of #58 among the world's pro golfers.

Race driver, Danica Patrick, considered the most successful woman driver in the history of American open-wheel and NASCAR racing, had won only one pro race in the fifteen sessions since starting her motorsports career in 2002.

Nonetheless, in 2013 she was the first woman racer to win pole position (fastest qualifier) in the NASCAR Daytona 500; has been the only woman driver to ever win an Indy Car Series race; and in 2009 finished third, among illustrious competitors, in the sport's pinnacle Indy 500 race. Impressive results!

NASCAR driver Michael Waltrip was winless in 498 pro race starts until winning the prestigious Daytona 500 in 2001. Dale Earnhardt, Sr., who had won seven NASCAR championships until his death in the same race Waltrip won, had, surprisingly, finished #1 in the Daytona 500 only once in his twenty-three-year career.

On September 2, 2013, sixty-four-year-old American swimmer Diana Nyad, who first attempted to make the 103-mile swim from Cuba to Florida in 1978, succeeded in her fifth and final attempt, and swam without a protective cage. Her motto, "Never give up."

Actor/race driver Paul Newman was still driving pro races at age *eighty-two*! He won his last two races before retiring from the sport.

In 2016, at age eighty-five, Ed Whitlock became the oldest person to run a marathon in less than four hours.

Josh Altman, successful Realtor™ and star in TV's

Million Dollar Listings: Los Angeles, has written a book, *It's Your Move: The Success Equation,* in which he points out that it's unlikely you will gain insight (into winning) if your inputs are identical to everyone else's. "If you want extraordinary results in your life, you have to bring something out of the ordinary to the table...even an element of being a bit weird, distinctive." Altman adds, "Make choices nobody else is making; see opportunities other people don't notice; and believe that following these opportunities is worthwhile."

What I think Altman is getting at is that it's essential that we establish our own *brand*, both personally and, if applicable, in any business we start. Barry Sternlicht, Chairman and CEO of the Starwood Capital Group, maintains, "Every interaction, every initiative, every decision is a branding moment. You have to create an attitude toward the brand, and then you have to enforce it with product innovation and service innovation that distinguish what you're doing from what everyone else is doing." He added, "The key to achieving excellence in any organization is to benchmark yourself outside your own industry and to benchmark your company against the best in class—not only in your industry but all around."

Often overlooked too are the simple, mundane aspects of a task. Legendary NFL Pittsburg Steelers coach, Chuck Noll, often challenged his players, "If you want to win, do ordinary things better than anyone else does, day in and day out." Having been mentored by Noll, Super Bowl-winning NFL coach Tony Dungy added, "By focusing on the small details—inches—we could reach our goal rather than coming up just short." He likened his coaching approach to the "consistency of McDonald's."

I would add that when you're facing an equally or lesser skilled opponent in any endeavor, you've got some room for mistakes on your part and can still achieve victory. However, when you're at the highest level of competition, you're allowed only the smallest margin of error throughout the game or event before you're defeated by your competitor who's simply not making preventable errors.

Yet another surprising formula for winning comes from the final advice to his students by Ivan Pavlov, the Russian physiologist who pioneered research into classical conditioning. Pavlov advocated that one succeeds by "*passion* and *gradualness.*" He explained that to reach that state of mind, we must first have an experience of successes no matter how small. We know that weight-lifters start with weights they can lift and *gradually* increase to the weights that challenge all of their capability. Smart boxing managers start a new boxer off with fairly easy opponents and gradually advance to fights with boxers of equal or stronger skills. In any sport, it's sometimes helpful to drop back and practice at a lighter level in order to regain confidence and stamina.

ACTION STEP: Remember that it takes just one person, one team, or one organization to prove that something *can* be done. Pick one of your most difficult objectives and document when and how someone else has previously done it.

#12. ON KNOWING YOUR STRENGTHS AND YOUR WEAKNESSES

It's essential that you recognize both your skills and your areas for improvement.

Dan Millman, in his book *How to Succeed in Life and Sport*, summarizes: "The essence of talent is not so much a presence of certain qualities but rather an *absence* of the mental, physical, and emotional obstructions most adults experience." In that sense, it's less about demonstrating natural strengths and more about minimizing elements of weakness. South Florida real estate "rock star" entrepreneur, Frank McKinney expands on this theme: "Most extraordinary people are often notable for what they *don't* do. They avoid vices: the common ones like drugs, alcohol, infidelity, gambling, and so on, but also the more culturally accepted vices like overeating, complacency, laziness, complaining, over-valuing social status, succumbing to peer pressure, and accepting defeat. Instead, they develop traits that set them apart from the crowd—things like discipline, steadfastness in their beliefs, introspection, risk-taking, willingness to say *yes* and working to make their dreams come true."

Author Paul Dickenson, in his book *Inside Sport Psychology*, explains, "Athletes and coaches are often so immersed in the process of physical conditioning and practicing skills that they overlook other ways to enhance sporting performance." Dickenson focuses on the nature of an athlete's practice and cautions, "Practice in the absence of a reliable source of feedback will result in little or no learning because poor technique may be practiced repeatedly."

In a sense, effort is the single most overrated step to success. Effort, by itself, is an unreliable predictor of outcome as that particular effort may be intrinsically inefficient. In coaching (for sports and for life), I've advised people to take the phrase, "I'll try..." out of their vocabulary. You either *do* something effectively--or you don't.

Athletes need to clearly recognize both their strengths and their weaknesses. It's human nature to practice what we enjoy and already do well. As I suggested earlier, a stronger benefit, though, comes from doing the opposite—embracing and constructively practicing the things that are difficult and uncomfortable.

For me, learning boxing during my late fifties brought up some unprecedented, age-related challenges to my stamina. I trained and sparred with a pro boxer in his outdoor ring under the intense Fort Lauderdale, Florida summer sun. When I thought I didn't have another round left in me, I focused vividly on how strong I'd felt in the first round. I pictured it so clearly that my brain processed it as *real*. With refreshing, renewed energy, I went on to the next rounds. The psychology of endurance in the boxing ring got me through every round—never knocked out or down.

In their book *Going Long: Training for Ironman-Distance Triathalons*, authors Joe Friel, a trainer of high-level endurance athletes since 1980, and Gordon Byrn, an elite long-course triathlete and coach, maintain that most athletes train the way they *want* to train, not the way they *need* to train. Friel and Byrn explain that ultimate success in triathalons is not about being "fast" but instead is about being able to swim *smart*, ride *strong*, and run *tough*. They outline the success traits for *all* athletes to include confidence, focus, self-sufficiency (taking full responsibility for their actions in a race or game), adaptability, emotional stability, quiet cockiness, mental toughness, and being appropriately psyched.

Friel and Byrn conclude that "Ultimately, the beliefs you have in your preparation, your experience, and your race strategy are the key determinants of your mental strength on race day."

ACTION STEP: In addition to establishing what you *will* do to win, look within your lifestyle to see if you've got any unproductive habits or vices that from now on you *won't* do.

#13. ON DELIBERATE PRACTICE

It's not *just* practice.

Many sports analysts have identified and stressed as highly important the concept of "deliberate practice." Anders Ericsson has defined deliberate practice as an activity 1) that is designed specifically to improve performance, often with a teacher or coach's help; 2) that can be repeated often; and 3) in which feedback on results is continuously available. Also referred to as "dedicated practice," this approach provides the athlete with brief, concise, and objective coaching on certain sharply defined elements of performance. Deliberate practice requires, initially, a teacher or coach who sets a template or structured plan specifically to improve performance and then provides instant and ongoing feedback to the student/athlete.

The student/athlete is reminded that doing what he or she already knows how to do is easy and enjoyable but is not deliberate practice. In his book *Talent Is Overrated: What Really Separates World Class Performers from Everybody Else*, author Geoff Colvin explains that hard work alone--hours of practice—can take an athlete or performer to basic competency but not to *great* performance. Without effective deliberate practice, performers with extensive experience often do no better than beginners, sometimes worse. Advancement requires that a performer be in the "learning zone."

The way our brain works, with sufficient practice of any activity, what we've learned gets moved to the subconscious part of the brain and we've lost conscious control of that specific activity. Accordingly, it's critically important in *deliberate practice* to maintain our practice until we feel that we've perfected it. Our simple focus along the way that we're not done yet in perfecting a technique or process keeps it at the conscious level until we mentally consent that we've "got it" and are moving on to another learning task. Neuroscience has revealed that our brain processes new material best in short intervals or "chunks" of learning, with concentration on one task or concept for about twenty minutes maximum as the ideal.

ACTION STEP: Once you feel you understand the basics of *deliberate practice,* teach someone else about it. You'll strengthen your own understanding and application of this concept.

#14. THE ROLE OF MYELIN IN YOUR BODY

There's a body substance, myelin, that plays a significant role in skill development.

Scientifically, myelin is a lipid (a structural component of living cells) substance forming a sheath around nerve fibers, predominantly in the "white matter" of the brain and in the spinal nerves. Essentially, myelin "wrapping" serves as an electrical insulator that speeds the conduction of nerve impulses. The myelin sheath rapidly boosts the connection and communication between various regions of the brain and transmits action messages to spinal and extremity nerves hundreds of times faster and more efficiently than occurs in the unmyelinated nerves in the rest of the body.

Why myelin's role is so significant is that with any practice, we are "installing," that is, wrapping and insulating myelin around our white matter brain nerves and spinal nerves to set up automatic ignition and action responses as needed in future performance. It's how a technique learned in your short-term memory, otherwise often lost, gets implanted in your long-term memory.

Myelin insulation occurs with practice and doesn't ever "unwrap" except for age or disease. If one's practice is flawed, the wrapping will still ignite and send an imperfect or erroneous nerve signal. That's why habits such as smoking, over-eating, or other addictive behaviors are so difficult to break.

The earlier wrapped nerve responses will always be there but they can be re-wired, so to speak, with an alternative and well-practiced new circuit fully wrapped. The key to building highly-effective myelin wrapping is constant feedback and correction while learning and practicing a new skill until it's fully correct. It's what the concept of *deliberate* practice is about.

ACTION STEP: Keep in mind that any type of practice, with time, becomes installed in your brain's memory (the "myelin effect"). Review your practice to determine if the best techniques are the ones being "wrapped" in this process.

#15. ON PRACTICING ALONE

Within deliberate practice, there's a particular value to practicing *alone* in addition to team practice.

An event in my own experience opened my understanding of a surprising and unexpected type of deliberate practice that's common among many top performers. While eating lunch outside a high school football field in Miami one Sunday, I noticed a young man, alone on the field, practicing moves and patterns. When I drove by the field again several hours later, he remained at his practice, still the only individual on the field.

Heralded research psychologist, Anders Ericsson, studied the daily activities of expert performers in various fields. He found, unexpectedly, that the best achievers rated practice *alone*, rather than with a group or team, as the most important of all their skill development activities. The "stars," so to speak, within their specialties typically spent five times as many hours as intermediate performers perfecting their technique by themselves. The best athletes on coached, activity-structured teams still spend more time in solitary practice than do their less-accomplished teammates.

Ericsson has pointed out that it's only when you are alone that you can truly engage in *deliberate practice,* which he has identified as the key to exceptional achievement. When you practice *deliberately*, he explains,

"You identify the tasks or knowledge that are just out of your reach, strive to upgrade your performance, monitor your progress, and revise accordingly." Erickson adds that practice sessions that fall short of this standard are not only less useful—they're counterproductive. "They reinforce existing cognitive mechanisms instead of improving them."

In her book, *Quiet: The Power of Introverts in a World That Can't Stop Talking*, Susan Cain points out that *deliberate practice* is best conducted alone for several reasons. "It takes intense concentration, and other people can be distracting... but most important, it involves working on the task that's most challenging to you personally. If you're in a group or team practice, you're the one generating the move you most need only a small percentage of the time."

What we tend to forget is the powerful link between working alone and creativity. New ideas, concepts, and breakthrough strategies rarely come from the consensus of a group or study by a team. Novelist John Steinbeck, in *East of Eden*, observed, "Our species is the only creative species, and it has one creative instrument, the individual mind and spirit of man. There are no good collaborations, whether in music, in art, in poetry, in mathematics, in philosophy. Once the miracle of creation has taken place, the group can build and extend it, but the group never invents anything. The preciousness lies in the lonely mind of one man."

ACTION STEP: In addition to team practice (or group work, if in business), allocate regular time to practice (or brainstorm) *alone.*

#16. ON SPICING UP DELIBERATE PRACTICE

Deliberate practice still needs to be enhanced in order to be effective.

Deliberate practice as a technique is clearly a key toward winning, yet is doesn't assure mastery and outstanding performance. Quite simply, the highest-level performers in any activity consistently put in more preparation hours than the others in their specialty or sport. Author Michael Mauboussin, in *The Success Equation: Untangling Skill and Luck in Business, Sports, and Investing,* explains that the concept of deliberate practice has some limitations and that it's important to distinguish when it works and when it doesn't.

Mauboussin points out that since deliberate practice requires that one stay in a cognitive state, constantly focused and concentrated on achieving perfected performance—fixing identified problems--it's exhausting and difficult to sustain. He adds that you truly become an expert when you learn to perform unconsciously and automatically, freeing your attention for higher-level thinking.

Furthermore, a performer's implementation of proper deliberate practice does not alone assure mastery and outstanding performance. Quite simply, the highest-level performers consistently practice more than the others in their specialty or sport. World class experts in most any field practice between three to five hours a day, no matter what they pursue. Competency in some fields of endeavor is considered to take as long as ten years of practice. Young Andre Agassi hit 2500 balls a day; pro golfer Moe Norman, from ages sixteen to thirty-two, hit 800 balls a day, five days a week.

A characteristic common to almost all "winners" is that they are clearly driven in their willingness to put something extra into their efforts.

Probably the best way to understand deliberate practice is to consider it as a necessary, time-limited step along the path toward mastery of sport or skill. Once a high level of technique and performance is achieved, when one's performance has become automatic, further practice maintains the skill level and personal stamina.

To effectively add a new technique or strategy to what you've already mastered, simply return to a standard deliberate practice routine until the new skill has been adequately programmed.

Neuroscience teaches us that the brain needs time to organize and consolidate new skill data before you can effectively apply it. The brain can fully focus on a task for only about 20 minutes at a time. Accordingly, short, frequent breaks during practice facilitate the mastery of a skill. It often takes 30 to 120 days or so for a newly acquired skill or habit to become permanent and moved into our subconscious mind.

When you've mastered a skill, "filed" it in your subconscious brain, and are performing in an easy, automatic way, you've facilitated a higher level of thinking in which you can consistently visualize successful outcomes and the direction of a match or game. Almost all winning athletes describe using visualization as a key tool in their daily performance. Picturing an actual moment when you did everything right—in the "zone"—leads your mind and body to recreate that outstanding level.

Author Geoff Colvin adds, "Indeed, the most important effect of practice in great performers is that it takes them beyond—or more precisely, around—the limitations that most of us think are critical. Specifically, it enables them to perceive more, to know more, and to remember more than most people." Winners see a losing moment as a learning opportunity and apply a strategy to fix any problem without blaming themselves or circumstances.

ACTION STEP: In addition to implementing *deliberate practice* into your training, set a schedule for putting in at least a few *more* preparation hours each week than your competitors.

#17. ON LIVING BEYOND WINNING

Your achievement requires a foundation of living skills in order for you to benefit from winning.

It surprises me, but what seems to be the most difficult thing for high-achievers to master is the achievement of a balance of *wellness* within their personal lives. As part of my life coaching, I explain to clients that we can't become fully abundant in *any* area of our lives unless there is some degree of order in *all* areas of our lives including health, family, relationships, career, physical environment, personal development and growth, finances, and recreation.

Athletes, entertainers, and other professionals who reach fame without understanding this balance invariably share the same question, "Is this all there is?"

Several years ago, a Houston Chronicle newspaper article announced that 65 percent of NFL players leave the game with permanent injuries; 25 percent report financial difficulties within the first year of their retirement; 50 percent have failed marriages during in the first year of retirement; 75 percent are unemployed, bankrupt or divorced within two years of retirement; and the suicide rate for retired NFL players is six times the national average.

Every year, some of the most talented, new athletes and entertainers allow misdeeds and indiscretions to sidetrack or abruptly end their path to stardom. And some established national figures, including business leaders, politicians, and clergy, invariably allow some poor choices to destroy their reputations and record of accomplishments.

How does one avoid the temptations and questionable opportunities that invariably come with winning and success? It seems to start with a personal code of behavior, values, and integrity. When you know in advance what you stand for, it's easier to make the right choices. Dennis Waitley, author of *The Psychology of Winning*, reminds us that "You are responsible for your present actions and, equally, for the direction of your future actions, accomplishments, and failures. One hundred percent responsibility for causing the effects in your life. Everything in life is volitional. We have choices and alternatives. Take the blame and the credit for your position in life honestly and openly."

Probably the two most critical skills a person can develop in their lives are *self-discipline* and *self-control*. They're related with the former providing a format for perseverance in accomplishing any goal and the latter for avoiding impulsive missteps in thoughts and actions. Nido Quben, a business consultant and motivational speaker, reflects, "The price of discipline is always less than the pain of regret."

One of the traits of character most visible and significant to others is your *truthfulness*. It's difficult for many to maintain honesty when they've made an error or when the truth isn't in their self-interest. Yet it defines your integrity and is essential if you're to be trusted.

I'll add also that there's a unique tranquility and resilience that comes to many from their spirituality. In our world, spirituality can be expressed and manifested in diverse ways with each paradigm of belief holding equal value. Learn what's spiritually important to others!

As an experienced psychotherapist, I can assure you that there's an almost inseparable connection between the mind and body. In fact, some mental health issues can be resolved simply by proper nutrition, adequate sleep, and regular exercise. If we feel good most of the time and aren't dependent on any substance to change our moods, the other wellness factors mentioned at the beginning of this chapter become fairly easy to achieve.

Sensible nutrition and fitness at any age clearly form the building blocks of wellness and, ultimately, of ongoing success. Fashion icon, Georgio Armani, in his eighties when asked why he didn't seem to age, responded, " A well-maintained physique is a great business card. Ideas and intelligence are what matters, but if you have a well-maintained physique, it's better...It's a classic ideal: healthy mind, healthy body. And at least for me: discipline. Keeping the body in shape requires effort. It's the antidote to laziness, which is what I hate most of all. And it is an antidote against the passage of time."

A personal observation about something I've implemented throughout my life: Successful people almost always allow time to get adequate sleep and they start their days *early.* So much can be accomplished in the quiet, early hours of the day. Wake up at least an extra one-half hour early! Be OK with some solitude.

To live well, we need to be *happy.* In Denmark, there's a cultural phenomenon called, Hygge, a way of thinking that embraces a simpler, present, and focused life. Hygge involves gratitude, a degree of minimalism, the outdoors, and optimism. It's likely the reason why Denmark is consistently rated the happiest country in the world.

ACTION STEP: Draw a simple chart of your personal code: your highest values; those certain rules of behavior for yourself and what you expect of others; and how you define integrity.

#18. ON DEFENSE

Offense puts points on the board but *defense wins.*

Legendary Boston Celtics' basketball coach, Arnold "Red" Auerbach taught, "Never rest on defense!" He explained, "I watched our opponents closely, and any time I saw someone loafing on defense, I instructed my players to run the ball right at him. When we identified someone like that, we embarrassed him. You can't rest on defense."

In an ESPN article, Defense Wins Championships: Consistently True," writer Sharon Katz pointed out in January, 2016 that during the previous year, pro teams with the strongest defensive statistics had won championships again and again: the Blackhawks won the Stanley Cup; the Warriors won the NBA title; the US soccer team won the World Cup; the Royals won the World Series; and Alabama's college football team won the National Championship. Shortly after Katz's article, the Denver Broncos, a team with a dominant defensive strategy, won the Super Bowl.

In sports, in business, and in the game of life, it's not enough to simply "put points on the scoreboard." It's critically important to protect a lead, to anticipate an opponent's moves, and to change course when necessary. When the other side is winning, it's time to show a stronger mental game—immune to intimidation and free of the anxiety that often arrives when one is behind.

Motivational speaker and author Marshall Sylver maintains, "Your success in life will be in direct proportion to your ability to embrace stress." Stress, whether in a game or in life, results from our focus on potential problems, i.e., the risks resulting from our actions, and our fear of an unfavorable result. However, athletes, performers, and business icons at the highest level usually handle stress in a different way. They realize that an anxious mind cannot exist in a relaxed body. It's a means of stepping back from an emotional impulse, taking a firm and confident stand, and putting a winning strategy into action.

At the most crucial point in a sports competition, the athlete who wins has often let go of the outcome of the game and has focused solely on executing well the familiar and long-practiced strategies for victory. In truth, when we feel stress, it should be a signal that something worthwhile is happening. It can be a powerful tool that helps us focus on doing what we do best. We need both the positive and negative experiences in our lives in order to evolve and succeed.

In his book, *Breaking the Habit of Being Yourself*, Dr. Joe Dispenza points out, "The real difference between humans and animals as to the alert-response ('fight or flight') is that although both experience stress, humans re-experience and pre-experience stress." In a challenging moment, we tend to think of the past and worry about what hasn't yet occurred.

In my sports car racing, nature bestowed at times the added challenge of competing in the rain. I learned early that many drivers feared driving at high speed on a slippery track with reduced visibility. A few even withdrew from the event rather than start a race in the rain. After a few rain race moments when my own lack of confidence seemed to be holding me back, I decided to fundamentally *reframe* my approach to the risks. I learned to relax (starting in my neck and shoulders, then down, gradually, all the way to my feet) and *let go* of the anxiety––a highly effective response to the vicissitude of Mother Nature. With this new advantage over many other drivers, I actually looked forward to racing in the rain.

In football, a quarterback typically becomes anxious and unsteady after throwing several interceptions. A kicker doubts his accuracy after missing an easy field goal. Winners, however, move quickly past these setbacks and perform "in the moment"—the present time, which is what counts.

A key point in sports and in most any other challenges: the crucial activity has to be FINISHED, all the way. It's not just trying. In football, it's making the tackle or recovering the opponent's fumble. In business, it's about having all the terms of an agreement spelled-out clearly in a contract, including what will happen if the situation later changes.

ACTION STEP: Establish in your own success plan the blending of defense strategies with the equally important components of calmness and productive processing of stress.

#19. ON RISK

Risk is inherent in our lives.

Actually, the most dangerous activity we engage in is the daily driving of our automobiles. Although we're more likely to suffer a significant injury or loss of life from a crash while driving rather than from poor lifestyle habits such as obesity, smoking, and so on, we usually don't think about the risk. Conquering certain risks, particularly when controlled and properly prepared for, can become both appealing and invigorating— the essence of challenging adventures in our lives!

The late international race driver, Bruce McClaren, said in a eulogy for a deceased teammate, "To do something well is so worthwhile that to die trying to do it better cannot be foolhardy. Indeed, life is not measured in years alone, but in achievement."

In my seventeen years as a race driver, I observed that my fellow drivers tended to be more alert, careful, and relaxed in their regular driving and in their lives in general than others. One who takes risks in a sport or hobby usually has learned the importance of details and has expanded his or her sensory input--*reading* a situation for potential problems. Inventor and philosopher Buckminster Fuller elaborated, "What seems to be happening at the moment is never the full story of what is really going on."

When we're in school, we're taught to achieve. But how many of us are taught the *defensive* or self-protective skills necessary to avoid unnecessary problems and to manage stress in a healthy way? Such critical skills in our lives, but for the most part we're on our own. Dr, Dispenza, author of *Back in Control*, advocates, "Unless these stress-management principles are learned and implemented, we will continue to reinforce dysfunctional coping methods."

Those who win in sports, business, or life have often developed a refined indifference to stress. It's possible to eliminate the likelihood of a "choke" at a critical moment. A world-class athlete doesn't slow down and agonize over what *might* go wrong; has already practiced under stress; uses a focusing mantra or visualization; and has meditated and controlled his or her breathing, ever so briefly, to relax. Scott Hamilton, 1980 Olympic skater, suggests, "Under pressure, you can perform 15 percent better or worse."

Basketball legend Michael Jordan reminds us, "I've missed more than nine thousand shots in my career. I've lost almost three hundred games. Twenty-six times, I've been trusted to take the game-winning shot and missed. I've failed over and over and over again in my life. And that is why I succeed."

Gary Mack, author of *Mind Gym*, explains, "One of the paradoxes of sports is that fear of failure actually makes failure more likely. The thought of negative consequences threatens you, inhibits you, and tightens you up."

Fear of failure leads to contracted muscles and shortened breathing. It overloads the system with stress. Mack adds, "Fear makes you play safe. Fear makes you play small." There is really no reason to fear anything you can imagine. If you can imagine it, you can prepare a contingency plan, an "escape route," to apply if it happens.

Handling risk has a lot to do with preparation. Remember, Quarterback Peyton Manning expressed that while there were other quarterbacks more talented than he was, no one "out-prepared" him. While he was the key to his team's offense, he was prepared, defensively, to protect himself, respond instantly to changes on the field, and to minimize his fear and anxiety when in challenging spots. Remember as well that boxer Mike Tyson hadn't seen any reason to study the films of his opponents before a fight. This lack of preparation in one area left him unable to successfully defend himself when the far less-talented "Buster" Douglas presented a simple but surprising strategy in the ring.

Also, remember from Super Bowl 49 (2/1/15) the stunning, final seconds interception by New England's defensive back, Malcolm Butler. After the win, he explained that he'd recognized Seattle's play pattern from team practice and films of the Seahawks games. Preparation—the foundation of a great defense.

ACTION STEP: Take a new look at how you view *risk*. Calculate it, control it, and prepare for it. Be bold! You'll find unexpected benefits and rewards.

#20. ON YOUR INNER GAME

You'll win by fine-tuning your inner game.

Advancing from "adequate" performance to winning inevitably involves change. The mental programs we've personally adopted in the past, by now mostly assigned to our subconscious, will influence our future outcomes for better or worse. Legendary basketball coach Bobby Knight maintained, "In all of sports and pretty much in life, the mental is to the physical as four is to one." When a program is holding us back, we can reprogram and substitute an empowering thought process instead. Just recognizing that a majority of our reactions and behaviors come from what we "recorded" earlier into our subconscious is helpful.

Taking the next step of replacing a limiting thought with an empowering mental directive is as simple as self-speaking a positive affirmation. For example, fear and anxiety during the opportunity to kick a game-winning field goal can be replaced with the affirmation, in the present—"I *am* showing perfect form and *am* kicking this perfect field goal." Using the present tense yields much better results than the future tense, "I *will...*" Gary Mack, referenced above, explains, "Sports psychology has been called the science of success because it studies what successful people do." Winners consistently use affirmations—"self-talk"—and visualize, in the present, successful performance. They never play *not to lose* but instead always play *to win.*

Elke Graham, Australian swimming star, provided the surprising insight, "In training, everybody focuses on 90 percent physical and 10 percent mental, but in the races, it's 90 percent mental because there's very little that separates us physically at the elite level."

Former NFL quarterback Chris Chandler cautions, "Most quarterbacks in the NFL can throw the football. Most are pretty athletic. The difference is in decision-making. The best quarterbacks are the smart ones, who can keep the game in perspective, and not let it get too big mentally."

At the core of our personal psychology, our beliefs drive our behavior and our behaviors affect our performance. We develop our beliefs as we mature, with some beliefs formed by constructive learning and others formed irrationally based on adverse events in our lives or misinterpretation of the significance of events. Our childhood often guides perspective on life as adults.

In *The Gentle Art of Blessing*, therapist Pierre Pradervand illustrates the process of psychotherapy: "With the client, together we elicit the meaning, function, and consequences of their beliefs." Beliefs trigger biochemical responses in our bodies—the "mind-body" connection—and set the tone for either healthy or dysfunctional realities.

James Arthur Ray , author of *Harmonic Wealth*, observes, "Your results in the physical world are an exact mirror of where you've consistently put your attention."

We tend to hold on to our accumulated beliefs rather tenaciously. Most of our beliefs were developed first on an emotional level. We then usually try to back them up logically to justify our positions.

By our mid-thirties to forties, when our personality development is relatively complete, we usually anticipate from experience the outcome of most of our interactions with others. We have mental models of how something should or will occur. At times, however, we misjudge someone or their motives or circumstances. Within auto racing, accomplished drivers don't actually respond to a challenging moment more quickly than other drivers. They do, however, read the situation better and make higher level choices.

As a racing instructor, I cautioned new drivers that it's less about "quick" reactions and more about buying enough time to sense any changes in the event and making the *right* decision within the last moment of opportunity. A key skill in mastering the mental game is learning when to modify an instinct, plan, or strategy, based on new information.

Geoff Colvin, in *Talent Is Overrated*, points out that in tennis returns, the average player focused on the ball, but the best players looked at the opponent's hips, shoulders, and arms, which foretell where the player will hit the ball.

Frank McKinney, South Florida real estate entrepreneur and author, relates, "To be the best, you've also got to be willing to remake yourself to fit the changing demands of your profession and your life." In my decades as a counselor and psychotherapist, I became aware that the solution my clients needed most often was to simply *let something go*. It was often a fixation on a certain belief, a grievance from the past, sometimes since childhood, a lost love, a goal that wasn't achieved. In life, we sometimes need to let go of something in order to make room for something better and more empowering.

To a great extent, our mental preparation defines our overall level of motivation. The key components of motivation are 1) direction (where we direct our efforts), 2) persistence (continuing an activity until fulfillment), and 3) intensity (the amount of energy devoted). Varying levels in personal motivation, logically, explains why some highly talented athletes or performers succeed in the long-run and others don't.

In summarizing the psychology of inner excellence in his book, *Mind Gym*, Gary Mack explains, "In working with athletes and all performers, I remind them that we don't know what the future holds for any of us. So why not act as if you're going to have a great future? Set your goals. Do the work. While positive thinking doesn't always work, negative thinking, unfortunately, almost always does."

ACTION STEP: Identify a recurring thought that has limited you and replace it with an empowering mental directive. Bring into your self-talk a positive affirmation to accomplish this change.

#21. ON THE QUALITY OF YOUR COMMUNICATION

The quality of your life depends ultimately on the quality of your communication.

I mentioned earlier the importance of the game you *speak*. America's best-known motivational speaker and author, Tony Robbins, emphasizes, "The quality of your life is in direct proportion to the quality of your communication." It's important to point out that communication is not just with others but also with ourselves as "self-talk." Our thoughts and feelings do not always serve us well as we talk to ourselves. In psychology, the "self-consistency theory" is that we act consistent to our self-concept and our self-image. If we lack confidence and self-esteem, our internal messages will contain scenarios of inept performance and potentially negative outcomes from our actions. Surprisingly, as I mentioned earlier, a simple remedy to negative self-talk is in the exercise of "As-If." The new internal message is: "I will act *as if* I'm at my very best."

Your image is a key to your effectiveness in communication with others. Your image conveys a sense of your potential and competence to those whom you're trying to reach. Your image is created by every detail of your appearance and manner. If you're speaking to a group, the audience will respond to how enthusiastically you approach the podium and greet them. In sports, fans notice how confidently an athlete enters the stadium or the field. Boxers measure each other during the introductions, before the match has even started. Watch how your idols or mentors present themselves and use some of their strongest approaches or styles on your own.

Author Carol Goman, in *The Silent Language of Leaders*, outlines some insightful differences in masculine and feminine communication styles among world leaders in politics and business. To a great extent, these differences, and the problems and opportunities they present, apply to men and women in the sports world as well.

Goman points out that her research identified the top three communication weaknesses of male leaders as 1) overly blunt and direct--"loud, overbearing," 2) insensitive to emotional reactions ("Men don't listen."), and 3) too confident in their own opinion ("Men interrupt all the time—as if their opinion is the only one that matters"). Among women leaders, Goman explains, their top three communication weaknesses are 1) overly emotional ("Women let their feelings show too much."), 2) indecisive—won't get to the point, and 3) lacking in authoritative body language--"Some women act girlish instead of professional."

Goman also suggests ways that women can project more authority and credibility: lowering your voice, particularly at the end of sentences and when asking a question; moderating the use of gestures; and speaking up. As former U.S. Secretary of State Madeleine Albright recommends, "Learn to interrupt." Men are encouraged to project more warmth and empathy, to stop looking for immediate solutions to problems--"Be a sounding-board *first*," and to lighten up their intimidating or overpowering expressions and gestures.

In professional sports, effective communication skills can be just as important as an athlete's performance in the game. Key players and coaches are often interviewed by the media for comments and game analysis. French author, Elaine Sciolino, in her book *Le Seduction: How the French Play the Game of Life*, maintains that all is gained or lost in the first minute of one's communication: "In the first twenty seconds, others will judge your look; in the second twenty seconds, your behavior; and in the third twenty seconds, your first words."

I explained earlier that it's essential that you have an exciting way to briefly describe what you *do*—a great story to catch the initial attention of a listener. When asked about my work as a life and success coach, I start with the response, "I help people to achieve their *dreams*."

Similarly, Christopher Dorris, author of *Creating Your Dream*, shares, "Your words are the bricks and mortar of the dreams you want to realize. Your words are the greatest power you have. The words you choose, and their use establish the life you experience." Winners learn to clearly and respectfully state their desired outcome, both for themselves and in their interactions with others. What they ask of others is specific, measurable, actionable, and includes a time frame for completion.

It's critical that you be willing to communicate an uncomfortable message *directly*. Say it as soon as you sit down to talk. You'll lose credibility and control if you can't simply get to the point. If it's your mistake or your poor performance, admit it quickly and suggest what you've learned from it.

Pioneer newsman David Brinkley credited a teacher for the simple advice, "The faster you speak, the less people will understand you. Take that to heart." He did. People rate speakers who speak more slowly as being 38 percent more knowledgeable than speakers who speak more quickly. When you're asked a difficult or sensitive question, a short pause before you answer upgrades the strength and credibility of your response.

How we express ourselves in writing, whether in letters, e-mails, memos, etc., creates an image as well. Jonathon Tisch, CEO of the Loews Corporation hotel chain shares that his first boss taught him a meaningful lesson about writing: "Never start a paragraph with the word 'I'." Tisch explains that if you look at a letter and see a lot of "I"s, that's a sign that the person writing thinks of himself as more important than you.

It's so simple but so few do it: get in the habit of sending a brief, handwritten "thank you" or recognition notes to those who've done something for you or whose recent accomplishment deserves a compliment. A handwritten note means so much more than a text or e-mail.

ACTION STEP: Describe the *image* you wish to present to others. List several ways you can communicate that type of image when you meet someone for the first time.

#22. ON KNOWING HOW TO DEBATE

At some point, you will have to debate the merits of your position or the point you're making.

I think an essential personal skill that's underrated in schools is learning how to effectively *debate*—to effectively make your point. In sports, you will at times have to debate with your coach, teammates, or team owner certain aspects of your strategy and performance—and sometimes whether you'll be kept in the starting line-up or even on the team.

In life you'll often be called upon to support your position—your preference for a particular political candidate or policy; a neighborhood or business decision; a rule for your children—so many points you'll need to justify in a convincing manner. Your explanations will have to be clear and based on evidence. You'll *win* in a debate, formal or informal, when you've considered the issue from the other side, have acknowledged their point of view, and justified your position as fact-based and sensible compared to your opponent's more emotion-based and unsupported claims.

A brief example of how to *hold your own* comes from informal debates I've had with some of my colleagues on small business and corporate taxation. Their claim was usually that "under our present system, both small-business people and corporations in the U.S. are taxed at an unfair and burdensome high level—a 35 percent federal tax rate!" After studying the issue, I concluded that their claim missed a key point—what the self-employed, small businesses, and corporations typically *pay* in taxes. From multiple sources of government data, I found that about 60 percent of sole-proprietors and members of business partnerships report taxable income of *less than $10,000 annually* and only 3 percent in this group report taxable income of over $100,000 annually. Among corporations, only 18 percent report taxable income of over $100,000 annually.

The overall tax bills at these levels are obviously low and don't sound like excessive taxation of small businesses and corporations. Whether you agree or not isn't the point, though. But to maintain a convincing debate position, I had to remember and be able to use the statistics. To easily remember them, I used the mental association for "60-3-18" (the referenced percentages), cueing myself that my first car was a year '63 model that I purchased at age eighteen.

In South Florida, the Broward County Public School system found that students who participate in their school's debate programs (now available in all middle and high schools plus in twelve elementary schools in the district) increase their GPAs and literacy scores by 10 percent. Nearly 98 percent of the debate students finish high school, and 95 percent go on to a four-year college. Businesses have recognized the value of debate skills and this background on a resume is powerful.

Job interviewing, not just at the start of your career, but for promotion, auditioning, or even advancing to a better sports team, depends fully on your *presentation skills*. Learning to debate significantly expands those skills. You'll be judged better by others, on any topic, when you can back up your position convincingly with *facts*.

ACTION STEP: Pick a current topic about which you feel strongly. Gather and list several facts (the more the better) to support your position. Then see if you can identify several points the "other side" might offer as to their viewpoint and how you'd answer them.

#23. ON YOUR IMAGE AND YOUR CONFIDENCE

There's a key to taking your image and confidence to a higher level.

It's a rare personal quality that only a small number of winners have truly cultivated: *charisma.* By definition, charisma is a personal "magic" of leadership arousing special popular loyalty or enthusiasm for a public figure—a unique charm or appeal. While often referring to someone in a leadership position, it can apply to anyone with regard to how they're perceived by others.

It's about your presence exerting a compelling effect upon other people. Most people who've developed charisma, I think, have in common an unrelenting interest in and focus upon others. They approach and meet individuals easily and give the impression of their undivided attention during the interaction.

In meeting others and projecting a strong image, one can usually tell fairly quickly if a stranger, co-worker, or fellow student wishes to communicate and has some mutual interest. I'm a strong advocate of the "Three Second Rule": Make some initial contact right away (*within 3 seconds)* if you see someone of interest. Make a comment--or ask an open-ended question—immediately. Draw out, though conversation, what is important to them, where they fit in the event or activity. "How do you know _____ (the host/hostess) of this party?" "How familiar

74

are you with this gallery?"

People will judge you initially on a smile, a confident posture, your apparel and accessories. Innovative young clothing designer Christian Siriano points out, "You could be the most fascinating, fun, *not*-boring, person in the world, but your clothing needs to reflect you—your personality, your loves, your inspirations. Take risks and take chances!" What allows you to win starts immediately when you enter your "game." You must establish a posture of winning—the first impression of you that others will experience and remember.

I'll add, though, that men tend to be impressed by what they *see*; women are more impressed by what they *hear*. In our culture, both genders respond to communication by *touch*, often a brief tap on the arm, a hand on the shoulder, a pat on the back. We learn about others and see if there's potential for a date through conversation. Interestingly, most people fall into one of two categories: those who have trouble talking—introverts—and those who have trouble listening--extroverts. The first impression we make on others will depend upon a fairly equal balance between our speaking and listening—with an advantage toward the listening.

How do I form an early impression of someone I've met? I start with a look at how they maintain their shoes—in good repair and a sharp shine is best—and, if possible, how orderly they keep their car and how they drive. These three factors reveal quite a bit.

ACTION STEP: Pick some aspect of *you*, which you can develop as your "trademark"—something that will cause people to remember you in a positive way.

#24. ON THE POWER OF LISTENING

It's often difficult for us to *listen* to someone for more time than we *speak* our view.

We all know *that* person. He or she talks to the extent that we become bored and distant from that person and don't take them seriously when they do actually make a good point.

Quite simply, you'll be judged better by others if you're listening at least 60 percent of the time and speaking no more than 40 percent of the time. That's easier for introverts than for extroverts.

From a success standpoint, the differences between an *introvert*, that is, one who is often reserved and shy—a thinker rather than a talker—and an *extrovert*, that is, one who is often outgoing, gregarious, verbal, and self-promoting, are measurably obvious. Our culture generally holds the extrovert in favor and encourages confidence, assertiveness, quick decision-making, and energetic communication styles. However, an insightful book, *Quiet: The Power of Introverts in a World That Can't Stop Talking*, by Susan Cain, explores how our society undervalues introverts and highlights the many innovations and timely solutions that come from the "quiet thinkers."

Cain cautions, "I worry that there are people who are put in positions of authority because they're good talkers, but they don't have good ideas."

I think that the highest level of one's achievement and their *charisma* comes from comes from a blend of extroverted and introverted styles. This is achieved with confident, energetic, and inspirational communication tempered by thoughtfulness, altruism, creative problem-solving, and humility.

In their choice of words, confident people don't begin with openers such as "Excuse me...Pardon me...I'm sorry to interrupt..." These present an image of insecurity. Never apologize for your presence. Have an exciting explanation ready for what you do. In my counseling, I've always stressed the importance of the words we select in our communication with others and even with ourselves. This is the power of our linguistics. When we use words such as "depressed, angry, frustrated, dissatisfied," we influence our brain chemistry and that of those around us. Negatively-charged words, complaints, and accounts of injustice don't endear us to others.

And today, what's really the biggest deal-breaker? It's a recently-labeled psychological impairment, "technology-induced dissassociative disorder." So many people have subtly become addicted to their smart phones, texting, GPSing, and social media to the extent that their ability to give anyone else their *undivided attention,* even in intimate moments, has been lost.

In building your image, it's easy to rationalize your approach as just *being yourself.* But that doesn't always work. To yourself, you are what you think. To the outside world, you are what you *do.* It's an effort of self-mastery to frame and package, so to speak, your best qualities for others. What others will value in you most, I believe, is transparency and authenticity—not only in your words, but more importantly, in your actions.

Probably the single-most dramatic difference between healthy and toxic relationships, personally and professionally, is the amount of freedom each person has to express himself or herself as an individual. Often overlooked is a gender difference in approaching problems. A man often wants to "fix" things. He hears a woman complain of or relate a difficulty and his response is "OK. Then do this _____ and this _____--and it's solved." A woman often looks at the process differently in the sense that she wants to be heard, share her feelings about the issue, and receive support and encouragement during her careful exploration of options. When a man discusses a woman's problems with her and tries to be her "therapist," or unsolicited mentor, that role may be unproductive. A woman wants him to just *listen*.

Those who meet and relate to others easily can be identified before they've said a word. In *The Body Language of Dating*, author Tonya Reiman illustrates: "Confident people walk into a room immediately ready to accept approaches, to make a positive impression...with open gestures, good posture, loosely held hands behind their back...relaxed...torso open." Reiman adds that building confidence can be as easy and simple as adding one physical display of confidence to your body language to your repertoire every few days.

While training outdoors as a competitive runner

over many decades, I often glanced at my shadow to get an accurate picture of my running posture and stride. When running on the beach across from my home, I noted my footprints in the sand and drew conclusions about how each step hit the ground. As a boxer, I gained insight from following my image in the gym mirror—we've all heard of shadow-boxing. Our body language reveals so much to others and, when self-observed, improves our own "game."

ACTION STEP: Monitor yourself in a few in-person and telephone conversations to see if you tend to *listen* more than you speak.

#25. ON USING YOUR INTUITION

It's a personal tool we're born with.

Actually, we make our highest level decisions at the intuitive level rather than at the rational level. Intuition uses all of our senses and comes from a deep part of our brain.

When I was an auto racing instructor to new drivers, I pointed out that the degree to which they would learn to use their *intuition* on the track, surprisingly, was a probable indicator of their likelihood of success in the sport. I think it applies in most of our life challenges. *Intuition* is defined as a power or faculty of attaining to direct knowledge or certainty something one has perceived—without rational thought or examination. More precisely, you just feel it and know it. Women seem to have an advantage at this and gain by giving themselves permission to use it.

On the race track, I put myself in a state of mind in which I was clear of distracting or stressful thoughts— focused only on the track and the race. I pictured that all of my senses were fine-tuned. In that state, I would get a feeling when a situation related to the other drivers or to track conditions was developing. I always heeded the message and responded accordingly. While luck was probably involved as well, I attribute intuition as the main factor that allowed me to stay out of trouble on the track all those years.

In his book *The Master Key System*, Charles Haanel explains that "If you concentrate on some matter of importance, the intuitive power will be set in operation." He adds that intuition often solves problems that are beyond the grasp of reasoning power. It's important to remember that intuition starts working in a state of silence and solitude. Before the start of an auto race, I got strapped into my car earlier than most other drivers and meditated and cleared my mind for a few extra minutes.

I'll add one caution about intuition. For some of us, our intuition is flawed by the influence of earlier negative experiences, now in our sub-conscious brain. For others, a tendency toward instant gratification results in intuitive choices that are harmful in the long run. It's best to test your intuition early on and evaluate multiple intuitive decisions to conclude whether they've been serving you well.

ACTION STEP: Pick a long-standing problem that has lingered in your life, clear your mind, and meditate on it for a few minutes, asking for an answer. See it, hear it, and feel it. A practical solution will likely come to you though your intuition.

#26. ON NEGOTIATING

Every day we're *negotiating* some terms of our daily living. At times, we're faced with an opportunity to negotiate the key elements of our career, our financial well-being, and our relationships with others.

Does it make sense that so many athletes and entertainers who've made millions still have financial difficulties and bankruptcies? Skill, talent, and winning strategies in one's profession don't often translate into successful decisions in spending and in investments. Even those we recruit to help us—sports agents, financial advisors, attorneys, or real estate agents, to name a few— often fall short when relied upon to negotiate in our best interest.

We're buying, selling, and negotiating—or *not* negotiating—every day, often without realizing it. These transactions are essentially *exchanges of power* between two parties. Even in fixed-price situations, such as in the grocery or department store, we often ask for the manager (who has the power) to make an adjustment we feel we deserve. Along the way, we gain little by complaining about something without offering a solution or by accepting every price or condition as "firm."

A buyer or seller gains power through knowledge about the product and actually in *applying* the knowledge they've gained. That person knows the details, specs, market value, prices and availability through competitors. With this knowledge, the buyer or seller shifts the balance of power, so to speak, by knowing what to say to whom, when to say it, and knowing how to say it for maximum effect.

The best salespeople have become fully attentive to body language cues, their own and those of their customers. We tend to believe and buy from those we feel have something in common with us, even if we do this sub-consciously. Accordingly, great salespeople subtly mirror the body language and speech patterns of a customer.

Confident people are usually better at interpreting the visceral reactions of others to understand the kind of impression they're making. Women usually have an advantage in reading body language but are more likely than men to lack confidence in what they perceive, and often fail to use assertive body language. In my own experience in communication, I've learned how powerful a five second pause can be before answering a question, raising an objection, or asking a question.

To be successful in buying and selling, you must communicate with others in a way that inspires them to give you what you want. Persuasion is inspiration, not manipulation. Winners reach others with a *story*, presented colorfully and with vitality. That story enables the listener (buyer or seller) to picture their personal benefit if they'll agree to what you're proposing. You bring someone to thinking, "This is an exceptional opportunity that I can't pass up."

How do you make someone want something? Author Neil Strauss, in his book *The Game*, defines the process succinctly: "Give it value. You show that others like it. You make it scarce. And you make them work for it." Many of us are motivated by social proof: if everybody else is doing something, it must be good.

Winners in buying and selling often question the myths about what it takes to be successful. South Florida real estate magnate Frank McKinney, with his "rock star" look and unconventional hobbies, explains that winners develop traits that set them apart from the crowd while maintaining discipline and steadfastness in their beliefs. He adds, "The buy side of the deal is always where you really make your money."

McKinney's point is something that I've applied for decades in my hundreds of sports and classic car transactions—I "Buy Low and Sell Low." If I've negotiated a below-market value on a purchase, I can always get out of it quickly if the car turns out to be unsatisfactory and I can sell it easily—with a moderate profit—if I can offer it to buyers at an attractive price. Invariably, those who've bought cars from me over all these years have come back when they need their next car and have sent their friends and relatives to me. Many times, I haven't had to advertise a car I'm selling—a previous customer or their friend or relative has been *waiting* to buy the next car I have available.

How do you "buy low"? In my own experience, *cash talks*. If I haven't been able to save enough to make an offer on a certain car or boat—even a home—I don't waste time going to look at it. I drive a twenty-year-old Rolls Royce for special occasions and don't use it for daily commuting. Recently I bought a ten-year-old, well-maintained, low mileage Mercedes for $3350--cash--from a private party who was asking $4500 for the car. A new Mercedes of the same model costs nearly $50k, and the cars are quite similar in appearance and performance.

I'm always willing to walk away from a deal rather than to pay too much. I made the seller of the Mercedes an offer that was above the amount a dealer had been willing to pay her. I assured prompt cash and let her take a day to consider the offer. I also reminded her that privately marketing a car to strangers does, in today's world, involve some risks and uncertainties. I'd given her reason to believe that she could feel safe with me in a transaction.

I realize that it's difficult for a young adult to save enough to buy a condo or home—not everyone has received a signing bonus to join a pro sports team! However, if you've paid *cash* for your car(s), furnishings, and "toys," you'll be in a better position to save for a down payment and, sooner than you'd expect, afford a mortgage on the right property.

Frank McKinney, whose real estate investing tips I discussed earlier, recommends focusing—and obsessing a bit—on a "niche," a specialty area that you've explored and have determined that it offers most productive results. For me, it was waterfront properties—the first one, just after my graduation from college, being a small cottage-style home surrounded by larger homes. Over the years, I kept flipping one waterfront home in exchange for a larger waterfront fixer-upper, eight times in all. In selling collector cars, for example, you might offer "Corvettes Only" and provide fine examples of that make along with your refined expertise within that automotive niche. Become known as an expert within your chosen niche of a commodity.

ACTION STEP: Practice and fine-tune your negotiating skills in one of the simple venues : a yard sale, flea-market, antique store, or car lot.

#27. ON IDENTIFYING AND USING TEACHABLE STRATEGIES

For almost all skill development, we're better off looking to a competent teacher rather than struggling on our own by trial and error.

You *learn* well to *earn* well.

Another South Florida real estate icon, Jorge Perez, wrote *Powerhouse Principles*, outlining in detail the strategies that advanced him on his path to billionaire coming from his origin as a poor immigrant child from Cuba. Perez stresses that in real estate, the *plan* always comes before the *property*.

The plan for an investment absolutely requires full market research (doing your "homework"), taking smart chances ("reducing risks is not the same as not taking risks"), and getting help from advisors. Perez adds, "No matter how perfect your plan is, it's worthless if you don't execute it perfectly." Anticipate obstacles that may come up and have options for resolving new problems.

Remember, I've explained that "It's all in the *details!*" Those seemingly little things that can indeed sidetrack or derail your intention if not attended to in advance. Probably the unbreakable rule used by high achievers is: "If it's not in writing, *it didn't happen.*"

Sometimes it's awkward to get someone to accept the word "contract" —they're more likely to accept the idea of a written *agreement*. In my own transactions, I tell them that it's always my *policy* to get agreements in writing. Next time a telemarketer calls, simply tell them it's your *policy* not to purchase items or make donations from phone solicitations! It's hard for them to ask you to violate your own policy.

At times, a buying or selling transaction is simply not going to work. Some projects will not move forward. Perez advises, "Always have an exit strategy." While guided by a clear vision of his goal, he consistently reminds himself and his staff that in real estate, what can go wrong will go wrong (Murphy's Law). Expect the unexpected.

As to closing sales, Perez demonstrates, "The path to a solid sale never varies. The product may. The target customer may. The ads, the brochures, and the sale pitch almost certainly will. But the five steps to the sale never do. In every case, you have to lead the customer along a road from getting their attention to getting them to sign."

It's up to you to create the spark, build them to having an interest, then having a desire, having a want, and, finally, having a pressing need. Pay close attention to the last one. It doesn't just have to be a need, it has to be a pressing need. It's got to be the one that gets them to signing the check." Perez adds, "I sell dreams."

Wealthy people under-promise and over-deliver.

Breaking a myth about selling, authors Richard Fenton and Andrea Waltz in their best-seller, *Go for No! Yes Is the Destination, No is How You Get There*, illustrate how a fear of failure holds people back. If a salesperson can see each *no* received and every rejection encountered as *empowering,* the successes further up the path are inevitable. "Hearing *yes* is the easy part of the job and teaches you nothing. But learning to hear *no* over and over again and to never quit...*that* builds character and self-esteem. *That's empowering!*"

ACTION STEP: Sell something you no longer need or want. Develop a sales plan: the points of value you'll stress; how you determined the price; and how you'll handle offers and negotiating.

#28. ON THE POWER OF THE WORD "NO"

It's one of the strongest words you can use and, surprisingly, often a good starting point.

Win-Win negotiating is a myth.

It's not that both sides shouldn't come out pleased with the result of a negotiation and a feeling that it was fair from both perspectives. However, it's the *process*, from a psychological standpoint, that can leave both parties short-changed in the end.

International negotiating coach and author, Jim Camp, in his updated book, *Start with No*, reveals why win-win is an ineffective, often disastrous strategy. He explains that the age-old paradigm of win-win is "just the seductive mantra used by the toughest negotiators to get the other side to compromise unnecessarily, early, and often."

Camp demonstrates how the best negotiators aren't interested in "yes"—they prefer "no." Win-win plays to emotions and to people's instincts and desires to make the deal—to make concessions and "split the difference." When, however, you invite "No" by suggesting the other side feel comfortable with rejecting your plan and share *their* ideas, you've lowered the intensity of emotions and have started getting to the real issues. As Camp says, "No" allows everyone involved to put away the need to be right, to be the strongest, or the toughest.

Within this type of strategy, an effective negotiator

focuses on being fully grounded in the world of the other party. What, exactly, is most important to them? Asking the right questions is aimed at building clarity in the other side's vision of what a different choice really will mean to them. Great power lies in the words you select to start your questions. Verb-led questions ("Should...Is...Can...Do...Will...") are less effective than interrogative-led questions, i.e., using Who, What, When, Where, Why, How, or Which to start.

The best negotiators never rush to a close, but always let the other side feel comfortable and secure. They are never needy, can walk away if necessary, and always have a mission and purpose that guides their decisions. Within that clearly defined mission and purpose, Camp cautions, it's important to create a blank slate in your mind that is ready and waiting to receive any new information, new attitudes, or new emotions that your adversary reveals.

In negotiating, selling, or just trying to get most anything accomplished, remember—we simply talk too much and listen too little. We win by listening.

Beyond negotiating, most of us simply have difficulty saying, "No." We agree to do something we shouldn't commit to or promise something we can't or won't deliver. Our ability to say, "No" gets stronger and easier with practice. Important, too, is that we don't really have to offer an explanation or specific reasons why we've said "No." That often leads us into an unnecessary and unproductive debate with the challenger.

The ability to *rule things out* is a basic survival skill.

It can be prioritizing and simplifying the number of choices on the table or just saying "no" to unreasonable requests.

ACTION STEP: In your next negotiation, practice starting with an allowance to the other side or person that they should feel free to reject your proposal anywhere along the discussion and to share *their* idea of what they feel would be equitable for both parties. It will move both of you on to a more productive resolution of the matter.

#29. ON STEERING THE BUSINESS YOU START OR INVEST IN

If you're already "Open for Business," as a sole-proprietor, self-employed individual, investor, or manager of a company, your tasks of productive buying, selling, and negotiating are part of but not all it takes to *win*.

Why do you think so many small businesses fail? It's not just about *money*.

Jeffrey J. Fox, author of *How to Make Big Money in Your Own Small Business*, points out, "The most important factor to the success of your business (big or small) is to *have* a customer. *Having* a customer is more important than the business idea, the management, financing, plans, or anything else. This is rule #1 and must not be forgotten or violated."

Having a customer means that a person or many persons will absolutely buy your product now or will buy it when the product is available." Fox adds that *getting* the next customer and many more customers is rule #2, and *keeping* them is rule #3.

Fox explains, "Your business exists for only three reasons: to solve a customer's problem; or make a customer feel good; or both." He advocates that if you are a one-person business, you must spend at least 60 percent of your time getting and keeping customers. "Companies do what the boss does, so if you are CEO of a ten-person company or a 100-person company, you must spend 60 percent of your time getting and keeping customers."

Fox adds that it's wise to choose *fortune* over *fame*. "if you are your company's product or you are 100 percent responsible for the product—as in the case for an artist, a one-person law firm, an architect—then *fame* (lots of publicity) can be an effective marketing tool. If you are not your company's product, do not seek fame. Rather, seek fame for your company, and your company's products or services. Don't get your picture on the cover of *Rolling Stone* or *Time*, get your *product's* picture on the cover."

Fox also comments that business leaders sometimes lose focus on the success of their own enterprise with too much time spent as board members of charities, professional organizations or civic groups. Altruism and support for worthy projects are admirable yet aren't necessarily good use of a business owner's time. Fox cautions that while technology and social media can be great, business *winners* don't let it distance them from face-to face interaction with their customers and staff.

He also points out that many successful small business owners achieve sufficient money to support their lifestyle yet have lost focus on building their company's equity and presence enough to make them salable to larger companies in the future. Just as older athletes gradually lose some of their speed and proficiency, so do businesses and institutions unless they institute effective ways to adapt to the changing market.

In a business text, *The American Workplace: Skills,*

Compensation, and Employee Involvement, authors Ichiowski, Levine, Olson, and Strauss point out that "Fewer than two in ten people use a decision-making strategy that addresses how their decisions fit into all phases of their life, including those that appear unrelated." As one reaches adulthood, it's essential that he or she become adept in accurate *framing* of any of the problems or challenges that inevitably arise and have their own check-list of steps to study and solve the issue. It's about making good decisions.

Jim Keyes, who was named President and CEO of 7-Eleven in his early forties, shares a powerful dream that helped him understand how he got there: "In the dream, I was shown that I had three gifts. First, I was able to adapt to change. Second, I had confidence that I could succeed. And third, I had the gift of simplicity. I didn't see myself as extremely bright, but I can take very complex things and break them down into simple terms—perhaps just so that I can understand them!"

In his book, *The Greatness Guide*, Robin Sharma cautions, "Nothing fails like success. Success breeds complacency, inefficiency, and, often, arrogance." He points out that many leading companies stop innovating and stop taking risks. Sharma suggests, "The more successful you and your organization become, the more humble and devoted to your customers you need to be."

Sharma challenges business managers and public administrators to "Sell your desk!" He advocates that leaders get out from behind their desk and have rich and meaningful conversations with their team and with their customers.

ACTION STEP: If you own or work in a business or are considering one as an investment, think in detail about who, specifically, is your typical *customer* and how will you *keep* them.

#30. ON SPINNING SUCCESS INTO ANOTHER FIELD

When you've become a "star" in any venue, it's easy for you to assume that you'll become similarly successful in your next venture. But that can be an unfounded leap of faith.

High achievers often end up investing some or all of their gains in businesses unrelated to the professional specialty that brought them fame. It's important to remember that you usually won't just hit a home run in these new enterprises, despite the optimistic assertions of a financial advisor or a financially-strapped friend with an incredible new business idea. Skills and decision-making that we've *won* with in one venue don't always transfer into other fields.

Within sports, iconic performance in one doesn't assure proficiency in another. In my auto racing career, I had the privilege of being on the track with the late NFL Chicago Bears' backfield legend, Walter ("Sweetness") Peyton. While a player, he loved sports cars and speed. After many traffic stops for speeding on Chicago streets and freeways, he took up SCCA auto racing upon his retirement from the NFL. By the way, the Chicago Police officers always recognized Peyton and rarely wrote him a ticket!

But as well as he'd dominated the football field, Peyton found that fame eluded him in auto racing. He was no longer a "star." In a race at Wisconsin's Road America track, shortly after I'd spoken with him, Peyton escaped serious injury in a fiery but avoidable crash, one of a number of on-track mishaps he'd experienced, and retired from racing shortly thereafter. He later focused on several business enterprises in Chicago and did well in his post-NFL pursuits..

We all need an awareness of our limitations. When investing in a new business unrelated to the *winning* we've experienced elsewhere, we need to do the research and rely upon multiple sources of information and data. Taking classes in accounting and investment makes it easier for us to understand what our well-chosen advisors are proposing.

The key strategy here is taking the time to exercise *due diligence*. That's doing research on the proposal and how similar ventures have fared, fact-checking, evaluating the validity of financial projections, and independently searching the background of the individual or group proposing the investment.

It surprises me how often highly successful people and organizations simply fail to apply *due diligence*. As I write this book, *Vanity Fair* magazine recently published a feature outlining how a Silicon Valley upstart medical device company founded in 2003 by a nineteen-year-old Stanford drop-out made a meteoric rise to a value of $9 billion or so and subsequently collapsed, with the founder's net worth, according to *Forbes* magazine, dropping from $4.5 billion to "nothing." It was to be a world-changing idea, and eager investors and titans of the tech industry bought into it—without *due diligence*. I'll note that the founder of that company is attempting a comeback. Who knows?

ACTION STEP: Think about a scenario in which you're starting a business outside your field of success. List the steps you'd take to ensure that your new venture would become a productive investment. List the types of people you'd call upon as your advisors.

#31. ON LEARNING FROM THE MASTERS

Those at the top of their game are often willing to share some of their winning strategies and beliefs.

Al McGuire, Marquette University's dynamically successful former basketball coach, maintained, "There are three crucial times in a game: the first three minutes, the last three minutes, and the first three minutes of the second half (always have the team warmed-up properly before the game and at half)."

Charles "Chuck" Daly, basketball coach of the Detroit Pistons and the 1992 U.S. Olympic "Dream Team," summarized, "In team sports, defense is the only common denominator to winners. If a team's defense is consistent, the team will win more than it loses, even if it has only average players. In basketball, the most important factor in playing defense is defensive rebounding. If you don't give them a second shot, you'll never lose a game."

John Cheney, Temple University coach, offered the razor-sharp insight, "The first day of anything is important. How you start (mentally and physically) is how you finish."

Baseball legend Reggie Jackson called winning the science of preparation. "And preparation can be defined in three words: Leave Nothing Undone. No detail is too small."

A collaborative effort by members of the National Fast Pitch Coaching Association, *The Softball Coaching*

Bible, outlines five mental strategies that create a winning game: Commitment (playing with passion and intensity); Composure (maintain control of yourself); Concentration (focus, strengthening the mental game); Confidence (believing that you have what it takes to come through); and Consistency (controlling your play, planning, and trusting in your talent).

Jason Karp, Ph.D., in *101 Winning Racing Strategies for Runners,* highlights the top ten: know your competition; visualize your race before it happens; know what pace you can sustain; have specific, meaningful goals in the race; control your nerves; run even or negative splits (run the second half of your race equal to or faster than your first half); stay close to your opponents; keep changing the pace on your opponent; own the process (know when to hold back and when to take control); and become your own hero.

I knew at age eleven that I'd someday become a race driver. An aunt introduced me in 1959 to young August "Augie" Uihlein Pabst, of the Pabst beer-brewing dynasty. He welcomed me at his small sports car racing garage in Milwaukee and patiently explained how his entry into international racing was going. Augie assisted me into a hands-on position in the seats of his winning Testa Rossa Ferrari and Scarab racers. He eventually became a racing legend and I judiciously followed his career. I read everything I could find about the era's other racing icons: Phil Hill, Peter Revson, Lance Reventlow, Mark Donohue, Jim Kimberly, Carroll Shelby, Bob Bondurant, Mario Andretti—many of whom I later got to meet. As a youngster, I attended races and observed the winners' techniques and strategies. By age thirty-five, when I could finally afford to adequately enter a racing career myself, I'd learned a lot by observation.

My own auto race strategy over the many seasons I raced was actually less sophisticated than the approaches of the masters I'd studied. Yet my way, a simplified composite of what I'd learned, was surprisingly effective— and lucky. I finished all the races, won some, and always finished well in points at the end of each season. Obviously, any time on the track at speed starts to wear out even the best prepared race car. In SCCA racing, drivers are provided one or two practice sessions followed by one or two qualifying sessions before the actual race.

I noticed early in my career that some drivers took advantage of all of the allotted practice and qualifying time. That was OK, but those sessions put plenty of stress on the car. Often, those maximum-session cars simply didn't later hold up for the length of the actual race. If my car seemed to be handling well during a practice session, I came in. If I got in at least a few fast qualifying laps, I came in. When the race started, my car was still running well and always made the full distance.

Within each race, I could see that the first lap was the most difficult. The field was tight, the tires hadn't fully warmed up, and the drivers were yet to feel "in the zone." Actually, a majority of the trouble and crashes in racing seemed to occur in the first half or so of a race when the cars were less spread out. My specific driving strategy was to drive the first half of a race at about 90 percent capacity and then a full 100 percent effort, driver and car both *strong*, for the second half. My strategy to drive the second half of a race at least equal to or faster than the first half was the similar to Dr. Karp's race-winning strategy for competitive pro runners.

If one piece of advice defined my approach to racing , it came from Rick Roso, a chief instructor with the Skip Barber Racing School: "Every accident (on the race track) is your fault. A good driver anticipates others, creates escape scenarios, and executes them when necessary." A bit harsh, I'd say, but mostly correct. I integrated Roso's admonition into my race driving and always had those "escape" options in mind—in my choice of lanes on the track, how and when I attempted passes, and in my awareness of the other cars near me.

On various occasions, I had to drive off-track into the grass to avoid being involved in a multi-car crash. Then, still at high speed and on a slippery surface, I had to artfully angle back onto the track and into the race traffic. After a few of these excursions and another few off-track recoveries after losing control while pushing my car to its maximum limits, I'd gained confidence that there was always a way to "save it." As the seasons went on, my self-talk was that as I'd always handled it and that it was inevitable that I'd save it again. And I did, certainly with some continuing luck on my side as well.

What worked for me on the track mirrored the type of strategy that would facilitate longevity and market endurance in the growth of a business or toward the fulfillment of any long-term objective.

ACTION STEP: Evaluate the documented strategies of those you admire most in your sport or field and apply or modify the one that will "define" you in competition.

32. ON THE MASTERFUL EXAMPLE OF SILICON VALLEY'S "T.J." RODGERS

As my formula for applying the best practices of my auto-racing heroes into my own on-track program illustrated, there's significant value in studying how the masters in a given sport, entertainment specialty, political or public service organization, or business have risen to the top. Their stories are easily accessible in our age of technology. Just as I did in developing my own racing strategies from the best practices of the drivers I'd studied, anyone can apply their acquired knowledge to upgrade and personalize their path toward winning.

Among our own acquaintances, on rare occasions, stands out a master among winners. This titan's path and strategies, usually self-mapped from the start, inspire us and provide a template for success in any venue.

Thurman John "T.J." Rodgers and I graduated from the Oshkosh (Wisconsin) High School Class of 1966. Rodgers applied his intelligence and his Midwestern work ethic to his studies, to sports, and to a lofty "map" he drew for his future. Without prep school advantage, he entered the Ivy League's Dartmouth College on a football scholarship. Four years later, Rodgers ranked as the top student in physics and chemistry among Dartmouth's graduating class of 1970.

Rodgers advanced to graduate studies in physics

and then in electrical engineering at California's Stanford University. He earned Master's and PhD. degrees and added patents for his innovative transistorized computer chip designs along the way. Quickly advancing with two established technology firms in the Silicon Valley, he learned while he earned, and in 1982 secured funding to start his own firm, now the Cypress Semiconductor Corporation in San Jose. Convincing a pair of major venture capitalists to invest highly in a young man's dream presented a formidable challenge. But Rodgers' supreme confidence and his precise preparation sealed the deal.

Rodgers led the survival and growth of the Cypress Semiconductor Corporation through decades of intense global market competition and economic challenges in the technology industry. Now publicly traded (Wall Street symbol "CY"), it's a $1.8 billion dollar company with multiple subsidiaries and nearly 6500 employees internationally.

In 2016, in order to transition his company into an era of fresh leadership talent, Rodgers stepped down as CEO. His influence and his highest standard for innovation remain. He's a Baby Boomer who always kept up with the times. In 2000, Rodgers told a talk-show host, "You have to realize that no matter how you manage a company, your method for managing the company will become non-functional, typically in a period of one to two years." Throughout his career, he recognized that almost everything is always changing, and our strategies must be modified and fine-tuned.

Rodgers' winning path has been far from

conventional. He's been known as "the bad-boy of Silicon Valley" with his razor-sharp decisiveness, tough standards, and eagerness to challenge authority. He's been an outspoken advocate of libertarian values, Ayn Randian philosophies, and laissez-faire capitalism with minimal governmental intervention. Rodgers has had no fear in taking a stand, and he's been willing to debate his beliefs with experts in their fields. His lifestyle defines the concept of mental toughness.

With all he's accomplished in the technology industry since the 1970s, Rodgers has maintained balance in his busy life. He's always been fit and has nurtured his aesthetic interests. In recent years, as epicureans, Rodgers and his wife, Valeta Massey expanded their avocational interest in winemaking. At significant expense, they constructed three world-class Pinot Noir vineyards and wineries in the Santa Cruz Mountains near their home.

Blending old world techniques with state-of-the art computer technology (of course!), their Clos de la Tech company facilities and wines have achieved international acclaim. Massey comments of her illustrious husband, "He never thinks we're there because there's always something more you can do. That's a goal, and it's always going to be a goal. He thinks that the moment you rest on your laurels, you're done."

I outlined Rodgers' story in detail to illustrate precisely how this man, my high school classmate, charted his course from the beginning, accumulated a vast amount of knowledge from multiple sources, outpaced wide competition and economic challenges, and applied smart decision-making to build a technology company from the ground up into a multi-billion-dollar enterprise.

Success doesn't just happen.

We can learn so much from today's masters, like T.J., and from the lives, victories, and struggles of the icons who preceded them. Make it a habit to study and become enlightened by their stories and example.

ACTION STEP: Put together a catalog or scrapbook of the stories and best practices of those who've accomplished the most in your fields of interest. Get inspired and motivated by them!

#33. ON FINDING MENTAL GYMS

Your brain can be "pumped up" in a variety of *mental gyms.*

It's not really about IQ. It's about what you can do to *improve* how your brain works. Calvin Coolidge pointed out, "Nothing in the world can take the place of persistence. Talent will not; nothing is more common than unsuccessful men with talent. Genius will not; unrewarded genius is almost a proverb."

Gary Mack (*Mind Gym*) stresses "Training your brain is as important as training your body." Our brain is an incredible "machine" that can process vast amounts of information almost instantly. But it needs exercise and *deliberate* practice.

The brain consists of three main anatomical parts with associated functions. The lower brain, the cerebellum or so-called "reptilian" area, initiates vital body and survival functions, usually below our conscious thinking and intention. The "middle brain" or limbic system, primarily the amygdala, monitors our emotions, including fear and anxiety, and, to an extent, organizes chemicals in our brain to respond to those primitive drives from the reptilian system. The "upper brain" level, the neocortex, creates and regulates our thinking, language, and "executive" functions.

What most of us don't realize is that only about 10

percent of our thinking and decision-making is performed at our *conscious* level. The remaining 90 percent is from our *unconscious* (*subconscious*) level of our brain. Our *unconscious* feelings, reactions, and decisions are the result of our earlier observations, beliefs, and response habits that we programmed (transferred) into our unconscious brain for future use. We end up, then, using the material in our *unconscious* brain in an automatic manner.

We come out thinking like a *genius* when we apply the realization that 1) how we feel or are about to react in a certain situation is not always valid or rational since the urge is coming from our *unconscious*, and that 2) we can effectively program empowering thoughts, beliefs, and strategies into our *unconscious* to use automatically and *win!*

It's important to remember that neurologically the brain has an incredible capacity for change. It's called *neuroplasticity.* The brain can quickly rebuild and repair injured circuits and can fluctuate between neural states. Rather than requiring years, months, or weeks, the brain can often make significant changes or accommodations in minutes.

ACTION STEP: Find easy ways to exercise your brain. Play challenging games, like Sudoku, on paper or on-line, play along as you watch the TV show *Jeopardy*—stretch your mind.

#34. ON MANAGING YOUR EMOTIONS

Our emotions fundamentally define our performance.

It's important to point out that the prefrontal cortex, the part of the brain involved in empathy, emotional control, impulse, restraint, and rational thinking is not fully developed until about age twenty. Parents, teachers, and employers often struggle to understand a teen's decisions and behaviors—it just takes time.

Understanding the actual physiology of the brain, once fully developed, is less important than recognizing how the brain processes information and initial feelings. At times, our initial reaction to or anticipation of an event simply doesn't serve us well. Certain primitive instincts may protect us but are not always a valid measure of how we should respond or act.

Dr. Joe Dispenza author of *Breaking the Habit of Being Yourself*, explains, "By the time we're in our mid-thirties, our identity and personality will be completely formed. We have memorized a set of behaviors, attitudes, beliefs, emotional reactions, habits, skills, associated memories, conditioned responses, and perceptions that are now subconsciously programmed within us."

Since the body *becomes* the subconscious mind, the conscious mind no longer has much to do with our behavior. The body runs on "automatic pilot." We make decisions and act them out unaware that the source of our action is a hidden emotion instead of conscious reasoning.

We can rather easily train our brain so that we are not victims to our subconscious and its related feelings or moods. Lori Barbaria, author of *Abracadabra*, encourages, "Think about what you are thinking about...Nothing is haphazard, there are no hits or misses, nothing's accidental, there are no mistakes, and everything that surrounds you has been on some level contrived, mustered up, and allowed by you. So watch your mind and your words."

Barbaria adds, "Every thought has an alternative thought cycling around it. Choose the one with the highest intentions. Power lives in what you decide. It could be in the word *yes* or in the word *no*. Use it in the highest way." Neuroscience, particularly the study of *mindfulness,* teaches us that the mind is quite malleable or open to productive change based on how we manage our thoughts.

ACTION STEP: Develop your ability to recognize the often conflicting thoughts that enter your mind when you're faced with a decision. Learn to choose the one with the highest intentions.

#35. ON USING SPORTS PSYCHOLOGY

Understanding and applying sports psychology is a must-have tool for the winning athlete.

In the 1990s, while a race driver, I attended a three-day seminar, "The Performance Driver," conducted by Porsche champion driver, Ronn Langford, and Indy driver, Ross Bentley. They had developed a comprehensive training program for race drivers that focused on the mind-body connection—learning or programming skills within the brain.

The development of psychomotor skills was their key objective. Langford explained, "Psychomotor skills are basically the result of programming in the brain (subconscious), which will produce a motor response by parts of the body. This motor response occurs at the highest level as a result of integration from the brain to the body."

Langford pointed out that psychomotor skills are programmed into the subconscious by many repetitions. The brain produces patterns of neurons. The programming is the sum total of what you practiced, whether correct or incorrect.

"If you practice the right things, the subconscious will recall exactly what you want to do. If you practice the wrong things, the subconscious will retrieve the wrong things," Langford added. His approach validated the concept of *deliberate practice* so that correct, high-level skills can become automatic, without conscious intention.

The bottom line--the cause for quickness in a race car—can therefore be expressed in terms of minimizing the number of cycles of this process of gathering information, telling the muscles what to do, observing any errors, and executing new directions to the body." Langford and Bentley's program offered techniques to stimulate the bio-electrical quickness within the brain and the electrical impulse communication to the body.

These techniques included "integration" exercises such as touching your right hand to your left knee, left hand to right knee, right elbow to left knee, and left elbow to right knee in a constant rhythm. Langford suggested gentle neck rolls in one direction and then the other, with the opposite hand on the shoulder; and "lazy eights" for eye integration, drawing "eights" in the air with either arm extended, thumb up, tracking with the eyes without moving. As a competition driver, my pre-race preparation included a few minutes of simple juggling with foam balls, clockwise, then counter-clockwise. This exercise seemed to integrate my right-brain and left-brain functions.

On this topic of integration of right and left brain functions, it's something that most physical trainers simply haven't added to their approach. It's the powerful mind-body enhancement of combining or mixing seemingly unrelated exercise movements at the same time. For example, a right-arm bicep curl performed with a left leg lift. This forces the brain and body to work together in coordinating the movement. When one adds balance to a different physical task, the body becomes more adept and stronger.

I earlier mentioned the aspects of neuroplasticity of the brain in reprogramming or in repairing damaged areas. Similarly, the brain can adjust to and diminish the impact of traumatic events, bodily injuries, confrontations, disappointments, and defeats. These life events can be placed in proper perspective so that they no longer cloud one's ongoing thinking and performance. Our brain allows us to be naturally resilient.

Interestingly, *travel* forces an unconscious reorganization of a number of areas of the brain, particularly the hippocampus, the function of which is to create spatial maps. This likely accounts for our society's development of *vacations* as a needed and productive escape from our day-to-day work and home responsibilities. Developing winning strategies, habits, and solutions can, indeed, be facilitated by a brief geographic change.

ACTION STEP: Start using a few mind-body integration exercises to improve your performance. For me, as noted, it was simple juggling of foam balls, clockwise, then counter-clockwise, for a few minutes before I drove an auto race. Performing two physical tasks at the same time stretches your mind to integrate them.

#36. ON PEFORMANCE-ENHANCING SUBSTANCES

Athletes *do* win with performance-enhancing substances.

In an intriguing book, *The Perfection Point*, John Brenkus, host, co-creator, and executive producer of ESPN's TV series, *Sport Science*, points out, "Everything an athlete ingests is a performance-enhancing substance, including spinach, milk, and brown bread. All contribute to muscle growth, bone strength, good circulation, and every aspect of physical health." While anabolic steroids are likely on a sport's list of banned substances, sugar and some caffeine, both energy boosters, are allowed. Gel packs that provide sugar in a quick-digesting liquid are routinely used by long-distance runners, and Coke has been available at most marathon aid stations.

Testosterone monitoring is difficult since this naturally-occurring hormone in our systems varies widely between men and women. Yet enhanced amounts of testosterone can increase muscle development.

An athlete's body chemistry is unique and can in itself offer a competitive advantage. A U.S. Army study revealed that "elite" level soldiers generally have higher than average levels of an amino acid called neuropeptide-Y, which acts as a buffer against the high-stress hormone cortisol. One of the most valuable insights I've gained in my decades of experience in psychology and sports has to do with the Mind-Body connection and how our body chemistry can be performance-enhanced by practiced thought processes and mindfulness as outlined earlier in this book.

Outside of our own body chemistry and diets, there will always be performance-enhancing drugs (PeDs) and supplements—some banned, some not yet banned, and some simply overlooked by a sport's administrators. The question is "If you'll do anything to win, can you fully own and accept *consequences* as well as victories?" Ask Lance Armstrong where doping got him! Many athletes have faced liver and kidney cancer, tendon tears, testicular atrophy, hormone imbalance, osteoarthritis, and, sometimes, psychological dysfunction such as "steroid rage," during or after their use of hazardous performance-enhancing substances. Some died as a result—in the 1990s, more than six pro cyclists died as a result of using PeD's.

High-quality carbohydrates, fresh fruits, vegetables, whey, and lean protein sources stimulate the body's production of testosterone and other naturally produced enhancements. A protein source such as a smoothie before bedtime causes the pituitary gland to release a burst of growth hormone shortly after a person has gone to sleep. Your body can produce the blood chemistry necessary for elite level performance.

ACTION STEP: Adopt the simplest performance enhancers into your daily routine: lots of water, fresh fruits and vegetables, whey, and lean protein sources.

#37. ON THE FACTOR OF YOUR BODY TYPE IN WINNING

Your anatomy in itself is a factor in winning. Choose your best sport!

But you might be surprised—5'7" "Spud" Webb, one of the NBA's shortest players ever, was able to win the League's annual Slam Dunk competition. His first "dunk" was as a high school junior at 4'11"! His particular body could make an extraordinary leap.

More typically, in *Perfection Point*, John Brenkus outlines the physical characteristics common to championship marathon runners: as light a body weight as possible without being malnourished; legs that are light in relation to the rest of the body; the lowest body-fat percentage along with the highest effective use of fat in order to delay glycogen depletion; a metabolism optimized for making new glucose from non-carbohydrate sources via gluconeogenesis; and strongly efficient respiratory ability to transport oxygen to the muscles. It's an analysis by sport science at its best—and many of these factors can be "fine-tuned" along an athlete's path toward perfection.

In motorsports and in horse-racing, the vehicle or horse is the performance *machine* and the driver or jockey's weight diminishes or enhances the horsepower. In auto racing, for example, a driver of small stature has an advantage since most cars must meet a minimum weight *without the driver*. Being the lightest driver in the field, weighing less than 100 pounds, likely helped Danica

Patrick win the fastest-qualifier pole-position in the highly competitive 2013 NASCAR Daytona 500 race.

It certainly doesn't hurt to pick a sport in which you've got some natural *anatomical* advantage. The late Leonard Cohen, for decades a most-loved singer and songwriter, often admitted that he'd been born with a "golden voice." We've each been gifted with some unique and expansive talent or characteristics. Follow that direction!

ACTION STEP: Take an objective look at your body type. What are you best suited for? Use as models high-achievers with your body type and note how they carry themselves.

#38. ON SAILING THROUGH ADVERSITY

We either face the adversity we encounter and move on or we retreat.

Obstacles usually don't warn us—they just come up. Among my many running races over three decades, I competed for quite a few years each December in the Palm Beach Marathon/Half-Marathon running event. In 2007, I'd trained properly for the half-marathon race but encountered a major obstacle two days before the event. My right ankle Achilles tendon tore--half its width. Surprisingly, it was on my "cool down" walk after a good run. This was my first injury in more than thirty years as a runner. The dilemma I faced was more *mental* than physical since throughout those thirty years I had finished every race: I just couldn't see withdrawing from this event. What added to my mental dilemma was my earlier mentioned auto racing history of finishing *every* race as well. Failing by my decision in anything, even for a physical reason, just wasn't in my paradigm.

Believing strongly in "mind over matter," I rested for the two days until the race, wrapped my ankle tightly with athletic tape, and limped to the starting line-up on race day. My self-talk was that if continuing in the race seemed impossible after I started, I'd drop out after the first mile. My ankle was brutally painful for most of the first mile but then the pain diminished significantly. My body's own pain-reducing chemistry kicked in and my brain somehow "rewired" the pain-receptor nerve endings. I finished the 13.1 mile course in a respectable time. My Achilles tendon took several months to heal and I returned to running.

Two years later, while training for the same event, my right Achilles tendon tore *again* in training—this time two weeks before the race. Well, I'd finished the half-marathon while impaired before, so now I just couldn't be stopped. I could walk very little during the two weeks until the event but again wrapped the ankle well and limped to the starting line. I assured myself that my several months of training before the injury would still provide me with the stamina necessary to complete the race.

I finished the 13.1 miles under adversity once more, and my race time, a little over two hours, was competitive within my age class. Again, though, I had to undergo several months of healing and was left with some mild but permanent impairment in my ankle. Was it worth it? To me, unquestionably, *yes.* Medically, probably not. Since those two events, and the wear-and-tear of over thirty years of running, I can no longer run long-distance races. I have, nonetheless, been able to run in a few shorter races, finished them, and easily *won* the last one, a 5K!

The point or lesson of my story is that our minds and bodies have remarkable resilience when tested by adversity. And to *win,* at times, we have to just *embrace* the pain. In 1983, a young, athletic businessman, Art Berg, was critically injured in an automobile crash that left him a quadriplegic. He overcame the immense challenges from his disability, started a successful retail business, and in the 1990s became one of the country's leading motivational speakers.

Berg put it best, "I thank God that life is hard, because in the pain, the struggle, the loneliness, and the rejection, we begin to learn. And when we learn, we grow, and when we grow, a miracle happens. We begin to change...While the difficult takes time, the impossible just takes a little longer."

In his book, *Forgive for Good*, Dr. Fred Luskin reminds us, "To play the game of life means we had better prepare for the clunkers that come our way. Our real opportunity is the gift of being in the game at all. We are lucky to be alive, and we have the opportunity to learn the rules of the game and play as best we can."

One critical rule that applies across all our endeavors, in sports, business, performing, and in life, is that the world isn't always as we think it *should* be. Life isn't always *fair*. Setbacks and tragedies occur. People and circumstances let us down and sometimes injure us, personally, emotionally, or financially.

Neil Strauss, author of *The Game*, reminds us: "In order to excel at anything, there are always hurdles, obstacles, or challenges one must get past. It's what body-builders call the *pain period*. Those who push themselves, are willing to face pain, exhausting humiliation, rejection, or worse, are the ones who become champions."

While some crises are inevitable, many of the high-profile problems and melt-downs successful individuals experience are self-inflicted. How many popular sports figures, entertainers, politicians, and business leaders have made poor and career-ending personal choices? What did they miss?

That quality that most assures success is *self-control*. The person who applies self-control with irrevocable personal integrity will always maintain the respect and admiration of those around them *and* avoid a career-ending or personally embarrassing lapse of judgment.

Nationally recognized television co-anchor and investigative reporter Dan Harris in 2004 had an on-air panic attack. His melt-down, viewed by millions, inspired him on a personal journey of self-help. In his book *10% Happier: How I tamed the voice in my head, reduced stress without losing my edge, and found self-help that actually works*, Harris explained that he discovered that the source of his problems was the very thing that had brought him to high achievement in the super-competitive television field: "an incessant, insatiable voice in his head" that pushed him to the top but also led him to make the poor decisions that provoked his on-air melt-down.

Harris's self-help search eventually led him to *meditation*, the most productive way, in his case, to rein in that destructive inner voice that had led him astray. He found solace in the wisdom of Eckhart Tolle, who identified that voice as present in all of us at those troubling times when we engage in a "ceaseless stream of thinking—most of it negative, repetitive, and self-referential."

The voice, Tolle maintains, judged and labeled everything in its field of vision. He pointed out that "the failure to recognize thoughts for what they are—quantum bursts of psychic energy that exists solely in your head—is the primordial human error."

Harris fine-tuned his self-help path with guidance from Deepak Chopra, who said "If you stay in the moment, you'll have what is called spontaneous right action, which is intuitive, which is creative, which is visionary." He was also helped by some of the 2500 year old principles of Buddhism. From Buddhism, Harris assimilated the practice of *mindfulness,* which he defines as the ability to recognize what is happening in your mind right now—anger, jealousy, sadness, pain, whatever—without getting carried away by it." Most importantly, Harris emphasizes, he regained well-being in his life by learning compassion for others, exercising acts of kindness, and restraining his sense of superiority.

Harris's personal melt-down had been accelerated by his admitted substance abuse. The concept of winning over adversity cannot be adequately addressed without taking a frank look at this all-too-common problem in our society. Actually, we are nearly all to some extent guilty of less-than-healthy dependence on substances, activities, and even the constant use of technology.

An old adage reminds us that too much of *anything* is toxic, no matter what—oxygen, water, sleep, psychotherapy, philosophy, sex—whatever!

In a speech, Dr. Martin Luther King, Jr. proclaimed, "The ultimate measure of a man is not where he stands in moments of comfort and convenience, but where he stands at times of challenge and controversy."

ACTION STEP: Identify anything that seems to be holding you back. Challenge your fears! Develop a go-to strategy for handling any obstacle or adversity that enters your life.

#39. ON THE NEW TECHNOLOGY OF WINNING

In the past decade or so, it's all around us.

Assessing the true value of technology as a component in winning is a challenging task. You'd think that our substantial advances in predictive technology, data-driven/statistical strategies, virtual practice equipment, instant video streaming, and so many other tech devices would have automatically "upped the game" in sports, entertainment, and in business. The NFL now has the technology, in a GPS sense, that allows a team to chart every movement each of its players has made on the field during a practice or in a game.

But watch any NFL game to see that the *human element* dominates as to which team wins. Michael Mauboussin in his book, *The Success Equation: Untangling Skill and Luck in Business, Sports, and Investing,* cautions, "Not everything that matters can be measured; and not everything that can be measured matters."

In his 2003 book, *The Art of Winning an Unfair Game,* author Michael Lewis outlined his *Moneyball* concepts about the use of better data and better analysis of that data to find market inefficiencies. He highlighted how the Oakland Athletics baseball team had found new and better data-driven ways to value players and evaluate the team's strategies. The "A"s built a winning team on the cheap by finding players whose skills were underpriced.

The team's unusual path to victory became the theme of the popular film *Moneyball*.

In 2004, the Boston Red Sox baseball team mimicked the "A"s' strategies and won their first World Series in nearly a century. During the next nine years, the Red Sox won two more World Series but abandoned the data-based approach in 2016 after three poor seasons. The team returned to the *human element* of player and strategy selection by their chosen baseball experts.

Author Mauboussin points out that we must remember that some outcomes, in sports, business, and in investing, can be predicted, but many other outcomes are the result simply of randomness and luck. He adds that when decision-makers are studying data, they can easily and unknowingly be influenced by their own *bias*—finding the result that they hoped would occur. Results need to be considered within the context of the validity of the research process. Cause and effect simply cannot be accurately identified in every situation. Too often, conclusions reportedly based on data are instead anecdotal—that is, simply the reports of individuals who claim benefit from a particular treatment or product.

Technology can be a quick, valuable tool for a decision-maker to use in analytic reasoning. We've never before been able to access facts and historical data as easily. Communication and networking have been exponentially enhanced by algorithms, bots (web robots), social media, interactive conferencing, multi-dimensional graphics, virtual presentations, apps, and all the other tech "toys" that young professionals use so adeptly.

Technology forces change, sometimes abruptly. Hollywood and the newspaper, magazine, and music industries have seen their traditional customer and revenue bases nearly dismantled by competitive new technology. The winners, like CEO T.J. Rodgers and his expansive and ever-evolving Silicon Valley firm, have foreseen the changing times and stayed ahead.

In my sport of auto racing, the technology of the HANS (Head and Neck Support) system has saved the lives of hundreds of drivers internationally and likely would have saved the life of racing legend Dale Earnhardt, Sr., had he elected to use the HANS system available to him. In the NFL, helmet technology is reducing the risk of brain injury and scientifically designed pneumatic compression packs for treatment of extremity injuries are rapidly accelerating an athlete's return to the game.

ACTION STEP: Take time to learn about technology as a tool toward success in your particular endeavor. Somewhere, someone's made it easier and better!

#40. ON THE DOWNSIDE OF TECHNOLOGY

What makes our lives so much easier and what allows us to monitor each step of our skill development can also hold us back in our resourcefulness and creativity.

Today, it's rare to see someone, anywhere, who *isn't* on their smart phone. Technology, particularly social media, is, for many individuals, addictive. I mentioned earlier the newly added psychological diagnostic category: Technology-Based Disassociation Syndrome. An individual with this impairment becomes dependent on tech devices, social media, or games to the exclusion of normal, in-person interaction with others—and is powerless to stop or modify their dysfunctional direction.

Author David Rowan observes, "We're drowning in information, and it's hurting our ability to concentrate. You have to be very disciplined to switch off completely at least once a day. Shutting down allows you to think at a deeper level and provides stillness for this kind of dedicated thinking time. It is then your brain does what it was built to do, and magic happens."

An easy solution is to shut down for a minimum of thirty minutes sometime during the day—no phone, no computer, no television. Leave your phone home for a morning or afternoon. Speak with someone in person. While texting and e-mail are easy, neither can convey the human emotions exchanged in face-to-face interaction.

Phone calls have the personal touch, and the human voice conveys intention more accurately than texts or e-mails. Reading books, the old way, in quiet environments, is simply good for the soul.

In his book, *The Greatness Guide*, author Robin Sharma comments, "The paradox of our wired world is that as we become more connected electronically, we become less connected emotionally."

ACTION STEP: Set aside at least thirty minutes each day during which you use no phone, no computer, and no television. Go out into nature. Spend the time quietly alone, or alternatively, in face-to-face interaction with others.

#41. ON LIVING RICH WITHOUT BEING RICH

If it happens to be important to you, it *is* possible to live rich without being rich. It's been my "hobby" for most of my life.

Most of us don't earn anywhere near the salaries of top athletes, entertainers, or corporate icons.

But at the same time, a Sports Illustrated feature on the earnings of professional athletes reveals that 78 percent of NFL players file bankruptcy or experience serious financial stress within two years of leaving the game. The report adds that 60 percent of NBA players file bankruptcy within five years of their retirement from the sport. We all know of actors, musicians, and business icons who've gone from the pinnacles of affluence to poverty.

What goes wrong? Often, it's having the wrong "advisors," self-serving friends, excessive spending, gambling, addictions, failed marriages, child-support obligations, and, critically, low financial literacy.

I've never been rich. What I decided to do back at the beginning, though, was to figure out a way to live large on a relatively modest budget. It took a while to figure it out and fine-tune the strategy, but I've stayed with it all these years. If it was just about the money, then so many of those NFL and NBA athletes with seven-figure contracts and salaries wouldn't be broke!

Wealthy people always know the *score*. They know

exactly how much money comes in, from what efforts, and how much, at any time, they're spending and the amounts of their ongoing obligations.

Since I figured it out many years ago, it's been easy to live an affluent lifestyle without spending any more than what's in most people's budget.

There's nothing wrong with aspiring to and living an affluent lifestyle. It just takes time and a disciplined "play book." Even for those who are fortunate enough to gain a windfall of cash early, their greatest vulnerability is in *instant gratification*. As Mick Jagger sang, "You Can't Always Get What You Want." I'd change the lyric from "can't" to "shouldn't."

Over the past twenty-seven years, I've owned ten Rolls-Royce and Bentley automobiles. But it took ten years of saving and conducting research for the first one, a fifteen-year-old model at that. It's called *delayed gratification*. During that time, saving and visualizing, I'd visit Rolls-Royce showrooms and learn about their previously-owned inventories. I was in the market for a Rolls-Royce—I just didn't reveal to the salesman exactly *when*. They all treated me with respect.

With careful planning, I was able to avoid the financial pitfalls of owning these types of cars. My play book beginning with the first purchase allowed me to gradually find well-maintained examples at prices somewhat below the market. Accordingly, my operating expenses for these cars over the years have been modest and I've usually sold each car several years later for more than I'd paid. So my actual cost of driving ten Rolls-Royces and Bentleys over twenty-seven years has been just about nothing. But WOW, what a ride it's been!

High-end, impressive cars don't have to be new. If an NFL or NBA player (or a model, actress, or entertainer) buys a *new* Rolls-Royce Phantom, the cost is about $550,000 plus almost $7000 in the federal "gas-guzzler" tax, and another $33,000 or so in sales tax. Insurance will add another $7000 or so annually. For the most part, my twenty-year-old $14,000 Rolls-Royce Silver Spur III makes the same impression, for 1/40th the cost of a new one.

While browsing in a charity thrift store, I recently happened upon a nearly new, gently used Armani Collection silk shirt. I recognized the value immediately and it was in my size. The shirt retails for $350, but here it was priced at $3.75 in the store's monthly "90% off" section. Much of my wardrobe has come from the thrift stores on the island of Palm Beach where I live. Why spend $3000 or more for a new Armani suit when a slightly used one can be purchased for under $100? Ralph Lauren Polo, Bally, Louis Vuitton, Prada, Dolce and Gabbana—they're all there. You'll find similar bargains near any affluent town or on eBay. Years ago, whenever in Los Angeles, I'd visit a small charity clothing shop, "A Star is Worn," in West Hollywood. Celebrities donated their unwanted clothing and the sales tags indicated who had worn the item. For years I enjoyed wearing one of John Travolta's jackets and one of Sting's sweaters. It made for great conversation!

Living large, taking trips to exotic locations, and indulging ourselves at times, as long as it's within our means, is exciting and restorative. But it's not all there is.

In her book *Why You're Not Married Yet*, Tracy McMillan's view is that, "No one in the history of mankind ever became permanently happy by getting what they wanted. It's impossible to be happy forever by *getting* something." I'd add that it's wise to savor the *wanting* as much as the *having*.

Tyler Durden wisely cautioned, "The things you own end up owning you."

It's important to remember that wanting and achieving wealth and symbols of success represent simply a *choice* a person makes. That path has obvious benefits and ongoing drawbacks. A different choice of placing one's highest value on relationships, health, spirituality, giving, or the environment instead of "things" deserves unquestionable respect and equally represents living *rich*.

ACTION STEP: This is an "either/or" suggestion.

If "stuff" happens at this time to be important to you, make it a game to get the most value within your budget for clothing, home items, entertainment, trips, cars—anything. Let your friends wonder how you did it.

If "stuff" doesn't matter that much to you, take time to look at some of the recent templates for downsizing and prioritizing the elements of your lifestyle. A 2016 film, *Minimalism: A Documentary About the Important Things,* follows Joshua Fields Milburn and Ryan Nicodemus in their modestly fitted tour of the U.S. to discuss this topic, which they wrote about in a book, *Everything That Remains*.

Either the film or the book will educate and enlighten you. If simplifying your life is a priority, this can be a solid *win* for you.

#42. ON LOOKING OUT ON YOUR WAY UP

Along your path to becoming a winner, you've added some new risks to your well-being.

Be assured that when you win, when you become successful, someone will be watching you, and not always in an admiring way. On Palm Beach island where I live, many affluent, normally careful individuals were "taken," devastatingly, by our neighbor, Bernie Madoff.

He cheated investors across the U.S. and internationally and fooled the regulatory agencies. Protecting yourself from unscrupulous individuals who've targeted you is an essential skill-set along with the personal game plan that got one to the top.

How could Bernie Madoff have been stopped decades ago? Simply. The financial advisors, investors, or regulators needed to ask the right questions and require that Madoff provide verifiable answers. It just never happened.

Throughout my career in the psychology field, I was intrigued with body language and had written my graduate school thesis on the topic. To protect ourselves from subtle deception, we need to accurately interpret what we see, not just what we hear. We spend years learning to read and write, but no one formally teaches us body language. In our own communication with others, as well, effective body language enables us to project ourselves favorably and with credibility.

One gesture alone can't be interpreted accurately but within the context of base-line body language signals, meaningful assumptions can be made. Actually, I've suggested over the years that one should be careful not to pay too much attention to the "shell" of a person's demeanor —it's often just the way they are—but to instead look to changes or shifts from their "base-line" body language. Likely, it's the new or surprising posture a person takes when asked a particularly probing question. It's important to remember, too, that many behaviors (such as excessive touching of the face or neck, or blushing) are often mistaken for dishonesty and are instead simply manifestations of stress and not deception.

Surprisingly, a person's face and eyes are not consistently valid measures of deception. The feet and legs are actually the most revealing element of body language. Accordingly, it's better to view a person's profile fully when sitting or, if not practical, to view them from their standing position.

For example, a person who finds a conversation or line of questioning uncomfortable will often point their feet and lower torso toward an exit. Security staff in retail stores know well that shoplifters will try to hide their presence by restricting their motions (less activity than you'd expect from a shopper) and often hunch over, unconsciously, as if to be invisible. They're easy to spot with a trained eye.

Many of the con men (and con women) in our society have innate or well-practiced skills in deception yet usually have some fatal flaws in their game. Predators and liars will often actually engage in greater eye contact than most individuals and will lock eyes with you. The give-away, though, is that most liars unconsciously hide their hands when talking and are less likely to have physical contact with the one they're speaking with. During deception, there's often an incongruity between the words and the body language. If someone's sincere, their accompanying gestures almost always come a beat before their words and not after. From tone of voice and pace, we can usually tell when someone is uncomfortable with an issue.

The particular words chosen by someone intending to deceive you are often revealing as well. When a person is fully confident and forthright in a statement, they're more likely to use the pronouns "I," "we," or "us." "Yes. I locked the garage." If asked whether they took the rest of the beer home after a company party, a deceptive person may answer, "Why would someone do that?" Similarly, a probing question may prompt a deceptive answer as in, "You're asking whether I took the beer home?" That buys a little time to construct some type of more convincing answer.

There's a unique aspect to prevarication or deception by people in particularly high power or of high status, as with Bernie Madoff. When people in power lie, they're usually focusing their intention on the *rewards*, either to themselves, their shareholders, or their organizations, more than on the *costs* of their deception.

In Madoff's case, he provided a lavish lifestyle for himself and his family as well as stellar financial gains for a

138

small roundtable of preferred friends/investors. He was as smooth and calm as could be. For most people, author Janine Driver (*You Can't Lie To Me*) explains, "...lying raises the toxic stress hormone, cortisol; power lowers it." A person in a high position of power is often consumed with positive emotions and confidence. While the common liar experiences stress from lying, sometimes fairly well-concealed, the high-profile liar spins a relaxed tale—often with a Teflon-coated conscience. How do you catch them? Demand the facts. When their statement seems incredible, simply ask, "Really...?" Pause, and then watch them to try to dig their way out.

Sometimes we need to protect ourselves not from deception but from abuse or control by others as well. Body language can help, particularly when we observe how someone (new date, boyfriend/girlfriend, business colleague, etc.) handles a stressful or confrontational situation. Their driving style is often a quick mirror of certain underlying aspects of their personality: calm, angry, careful, aggressive?

So often, otherwise successful people are less skilled when it comes to protecting themselves from lapses of integrity by others. It's about watching for the incongruent signals, asking the right questions, firmly getting complete and valid answers, and following your intuition, your inner-voice.

With that said, it's important to remember that despite our observational skills and vigilance, any of us can be victimized. Just ask any of my financially-experienced Palm Beach neighbors who invested with Madoff. As time goes by, we could be caught off guard and may lapse briefly in our protective measures. We need the *due diligence* outlined earlier. Our awareness and vigilance must be "on" 24/7!

ACTION STEP: Practice watching for signs of deception. If you suspect someone is not being truthful with you, keep asking questions. Observe their body language as they answer.

#43. ON ESTABLISHING YOUR PRIORITIES

We don't always get it right.

In a heart-felt letter to his son, also a former journalist and executive with the Hazelton Foundation in Minnesota, beloved journalist Bill Moyers cautioned, "I worked too hard and thought too much about my work in the beginning to go on long walks with my wife, or learn to grow roses, or watch the sun set, or spend time with good friends. There are some things the loss of which success doesn't compensate for, and one of them is the joy of being with someone you love and in awe of life itself."

When you're *winning*, it's easy to lose track of the *balance* that is so essential in our lives.

As a psychotherapist, life coach, and escort to affluent people—particularly in the rarified and dazzling environment of Palm Beach—I've seen a common factor among those who've lost that *balance* in their lives. It seems to come from an *exaggerated focus on self-interest.* Quite simply, many successful people *want to do what they want to do.* They'll persist, cajole, lobby, or file lawsuits simply to get their way—even if it's not in the equitable interest of others or the public. Why? Because they *can.*

Psychologically, having to *win* at any expense, always, is an immature way to look at life. If it's about wealth, the truth is that with all the opportunities available to each of us, making money, even establishing a brand, is fairly easy (particularly if you follow some of the concepts in this book!). What is more difficult, though, is building *character*. If you can become a person who is consistently fair and who speaks and acts with consideration of others, even your adversaries and the critics of your decisions will maintain respect for you as a person.

George Bernard Shaw said, "The reasonable man adapts himself to the world, the unreasonable one persists in trying to adapt the world to himself. Therefore, all progress depends on the unreasonable." That's an anthem in the pursuit of self-interest and to an extent, it works. What's lost, though, in an unbalanced focus on self-interest is that from a quantum physics standpoint we are all molecularly part of one world. For harmony in that world, what's good for one of us needs to be aligned with what's in the best interest of others as well. It does all seem to get sorted out in the end and that's the reason why some stars inevitably fall from grace.

ACTION STEP: Ask yourself what the most important priorities in your life *really* are. Learn to recognize when your focus has shifted only to your own *self-interest* and grade yourself on your fairness and respect for others.

44. ON THE PERFORMANCE MAGIC OF DISNEY

Disney has developed some unique and teachable strategies for winning.

Lee Cockerell, former Executive Vice President of Operations at the Walt Disney Resort, has shared in his book, *Creating Magic*, the key leadership strategies that have enabled Disney to win and win again over so many years. "It's not the magic that makes it work; it's the way we work that makes it magic." Cockerell points out, *"Everyone is important"* and that your people make your brand.

How does Disney maintain high-quality service at its parks and resorts? Each of the 59,000 cast members is trained to treat each and every guest with the utmost care and respect. They do this because they are treated exactly the same way by the Disney leadership.

Disney lets it be known that managers and executives are evaluated not only on their bottom-line results but on *how* those results were obtained. Cockerell goes on to explain that when *everyone* matters, employees are happy to come to work, and they're eager to give you their energy, creativity, and loyalty. "To put it simply, all people want exactly what you want. You want to be included, listened to, respected, and involved. Don't you?"

Cockerell adds, "Forget about the chain of

command. The days of the vertical chain of command as a way of doing business are over. Leaders who continue to manage this way are doomed to failure, because a rigid top-down command structure can slow communication significantly and deliver less reliable information." The alternative is to "get as flat as you can." Disney has minimized the number of layers in the organization so that executives can deal directly with as many people as possible.

Disney has some hiring criteria that can be of high value throughout business, sports, and professional organizations. They take time to define the *perfect* candidate. Exactly what qualities do you want in the person you hire? Disney looks for individuals who are 1) technically competent, 2) disciplined, self-controlled, and organized, 3) aware of and able to use their field's *technologies* to assist in the performance of their assignments, and 4) possessing *leadership* competence.

Cockerell instructs, also, that an organization must be able to recognize when the job doesn't fit the talent. In sports or in business, that #1 draft pick or well-endorsed new Ivy League graduate may not turn out to be right for your team or company and it's time to move on.

ACTION STEP: Visit any Disney property to see the obvious signs of quality, efficiency, and full focus on each guest. If you aren't able to visit, read one of the many books about the Disney philosophy of doing business.

#45. ON REINVENTING YOURSELF FOR THE BETTER

Over the years, I've spoken to groups many times on this particular topic. I've shown audiences that each of us has memorized, in a sense, a select set of behaviors, beliefs, attitudes, emotional reactions, and responses that we've programmed into our personality and our subconscious mind.

By our mid thirties to forties or so, these underlying patterns have subtly directed almost all of our thoughts and actions. These mental models can, however, be modified or replaced anytime—and at any age. Going in a different direction in your life starts *here*—changing the existing patterns. The saddest words in the English language are: "If only…"

Changing yourself for the better can focus on anything. Maybe giving up an undesirable habit, becoming more responsible with your finances, avoiding anger, spending more time with your loved ones—whatever you wish to improve.

I suggest that someone wanting to change, to *reinvent* themselves, follow their inner "gyroscope," the intuitive power of which I referenced earlier in this book. I add that it's essential to bring your *body* into the equation. Physical activity stimulates your mental processes and creativity. Actually, any change in your physical position facilitates a change in your (or anyone's) thinking. If you're "stuck" on something and need a breakthrough, change chairs, move to a different room or outdoors, talk to someone side-by-side instead of head-on—it all works!

ACTION STEP: Every few years, do an inventory of whether it's time to reinvent yourself with regard to some (or all) aspects of your life.

#46. ON TAKING YOURSELF TOO SERIOUSLY

Hunter S. Thompson's motto was, "Life should not be a journey to the grave with the intention of arriving safely in a pretty and well-preserved body, but rather to skid broadside in a cloud of smoke, thoroughly used up, totally worn out, and loudly proclaiming, *"Wow! What a Ride!"*

In our lives, putting in all that it takes to *win* does, indeed, leave us mentally and physically spent for the time being. Unwinding, taking a break from everything, and enjoying life's humorous moments is restorative.

Important, too, is that we don't always have to meet other people's standards or expectations. It's OK to embrace the beautiful differences, sometimes inconsistencies, within our personalities and lifestyles.

Author Gina Amaro Rudan, in her book, *Practical Genius: The Real Smarts You Need to Get Your Talents and Passions Working for YOU*, shares, "You can't be all things to all people, but you can be everything that matters to a key few." Rudan references the point of Dr. Christiane Northrup, an internationally-known women's health and wellness proponent, that, "The intellect always wants to believe that it's in control, and it isn't. The spirit is in control. And the spirit is where genius comes from, and spirit resides in the heart."

ACTION STEP: Vow to often take time to just *relax*, to enjoy humor, and to escape, briefly, from other people's expectations of you.

#47. ON KEEPING WINNING IN PROPER PERSPECTIVE

With all I've shared about "Who Wins and Why," there's still another unimpeachable truth about winning. Tim Laurence, author of *The Hoffman Process* and endorsed internationally as a leading trainer on personal transformation, cautions, "Winning is fine but only a small percentage of individuals can win in any given scenario." That's a fact.

Only one NFL team among thirty-six—all with expensive professional talent—wins the Super Bowl. Roughly four million kids play sports in grade school, middle school, or high school. But only a few hundred go on to become pro athletes.

Winners at the highest levels have been self-guided by stellar aspirations and confidence but are invariably aware that their accomplishments are hard-won and that their longevity on top—whether in sports, business, or in the game of life—is never certain.

Jay Wright of Villanova has become one of college basketball's highest-ranked coaches but he motivates his players in a very different way than other coaches. He stresses a "HUMBLE AND HUNGRY" attitude. Wright helps his players learn to be *unaffected* by the last play and to play for one another rather than for the adulation of winning. A sign in the locker room reads, "PLAYERS PLAY FOR THEIR TEAMMATES AND COACHES; ACTORS PLAY FOR THE CROWD."

One of Wright's assistants, Jim Brennan, is a motivational devotee to the concept that *resilience* is a greater predictor of success than talent. He illustrated that point with, "I don't know if we can win another national championship without another really tough loss. Like one that just kills you." A loss forces your attention on improvement and only then can you *win*!

How we frame success as an objective and how we handle whatever we *don't* win has a lot to do with our ultimate happiness and self-esteem. In my first auto race as a novice driver, I finished *last*—and to me, that still was a *win*. I'd made no critical mistakes, had no problems, and I'd kept the pace. But I vowed never to finish last again. Over my seventeen-year racing career, that prophesy was fulfilled.

ACTION STEP: Look back on something you didn't win and list several ways you were able to benefit from the experience.

48. ON WHAT YOU'D DO DIFFERENTLY IF YOU WERE YOUNG AGAIN

Here's what I would focus upon more intently if I were to start over. You make your own list.

* Useful self-control (resisting impulsive decisions)

* Inner compromise (finding a balance between what I want and what's practical)

* Unconditional regard for others (humility and respectfulness)

*Self-reliance (acting independently, without pressure from others)

* Becoming able to accurately identify alternatives (seeing more than one choice or solution)

ACTION STEP: State for yourself what you'd place value on if you were young again. What you write will reveal the wisdom you've gained and the qualities you can still apply in the remaining years of your life.

49. ON THINKING LIKE AN "ELITE WARRIOR"—THE NAVY SEAL WAY

Mark Divine, retired commander with the U.S. Navy SEALs, wrote a book, *The Way of the SEAL*, which outlines the exercises, meditations, and focusing techniques to train your mind for mental toughness, emotional resilience, and uncanny intuition. A foundation for his concepts is "Do today what others *won't* so you can achieve tomorrow what others *can't.*"

Add to that the mantra, "Success seems largely a matter of hanging on after others have let go."

Divine explains that we all need a set point, a fixed point on your internal reality map, that will help you navigate when the path forward isn't clear or when challenges arise. Establishing a set-point requires you to: make a stand; find a purpose; embrace risk, loss, and failure—they're often the necessary steps toward victory. Divine adds, "Connect every action to your set-point so you can answer the question, 'Why am I doing this?'"

SEAL's selection of high-value targets bullet-proofs their mission because they'll know exactly where their resources are best directed.

Divine advocates an exercise of bringing the challenges to you. He suggests at least one minor challenge for yourself each week and building on this new habit to gain strength for bigger challenges. The SEAL keys for mental toughness are: controlling your response; controlling your attention; developing emotional resilience; and visualizing powerfully.

ACTION STEP: Define a personal set point from which you can always gain direction when in crisis or when challenged.

#50. ON USING A "BUCKET THEORY" FOR YOUR PRIORITIES

Author Machen MacDonald, in his book *Provoking Your Brilliance*, offers a highly useful formula for determining how much time and effort to put into any daily problem or challenge. Overall, *winners* have become adept at quickly deciding what is the most important use of their time.

MacDonald's theory is that in your "bucket" of daily choices for *spending* your time (after all, your time is an investment), you should spend 85 percent or more on situations in which you have total control of changing and improving the situation; 10-15 percent of your time on situations over which you don't have decision-making power but you *do* have influence on the process; and less than 5 percent of your time on situations over which you have no control, decision-making authority, or influence.

I think that the concepts of *deliberate practice* that I outlined as the foundational key toward acquiring the highest level of sports skills can be applied as well to our skillset for handling life challenges. We can prioritize the strategies and responses that will, with practice, automatically come into play when we most need them— deliberate and intentional.

A meditation coach, Jon Kabot Zinn, advocates that each of his students ask, "What is it on this planet that needs doing, that I know something about, that probably won't get done unless I take responsibility for it?"

ACTION STEP: Each day, when problems and issues face you, prioritize and spend 85 percent or more of your time on those that you actually have control of changing or improving.

CONCLUSION

if I had to pick a short list of the essential insights about *winning* that I've outlined, I'd start with a reminder of author Marshall Sylver's admonition, "People say that you can learn from your own mistakes. That's true, but I'd rather learn from others' mistakes and let them deal with the consequences for me."

Secondly, I'd point to a Yale University study in the 1950s that asked the graduating class how many of them had a clear, specific set of goals with a written plan for their accomplishment. Answer: Less than 3 percent. Twenty years later, the "Goals" people were clearly happier about their lives, direction, and accomplishments and made more money than the remaining 97 percent.

Third, I'd caution anyone to be accurate in attributing both your successes and your failures. When people are asked to explain what happened, they are seven times more likely to focus on the significance of their efforts when describing a win or success as they are when describing a loss or failure. It's easy to blame someone or something else.

Fourth, from my real-world background in psychology, I'd add my difficult but inevitably true observation that a small but identifiable number of the people we choose to--or have to--interact with are essentially dysfunctional, even if they've risen to the top.

They may be unethical, rude, intimidating, or even abusive—and they've been able to get away with it.

We *win* over intimidation by these individuals first, by recognizing their *type*, and secondly, by preparing protective strategies to assure that they don't succeed in "taking all the chips." We win by holding people at any level of accomplishment or authority accountable to the *truth*.

In 1973, Robert Ringer authored a remarkably successful book, *Winning Through Intimidation*, which, surprisingly, wasn't at all about learning to intimidate others. Instead, the book outlined how you can avoid the mental lapses that cause you to fall victim to intimidation. Ringer has since written several additional "out-of-the-box" but highly useful books on business success.

Your own victory depends on your ability to simply say "No" to unreasonable demands or individuals. When dealing with difficult people, I ask myself, "What can I do to bring out their best?" Often my "No" has gained their reluctant respect. With some guidance and constructive direction, one's dysfunctional behavior can sometimes be turned into honest and transparent communication. Sometimes, as a therapist, I've had to remind a "star" that no one actually became successful *alone*. We all live on the good graces of others. We have to *earn* their positive regard and support.

Fifth, as our thoughts come up, day to day, in competition, crisis—in any other important endeavor—remember author Lori Barbaria's (*Abracadabra*) invocation, "Every thought has an alternative thought cycling around it; choose the one with the right intentions. Power lives in what you decide. It could be in the word *yes* or the word *no*."

As Jimi Hendrix said, "When the power of love overcomes the love of power, the world will know peace."

Sixth, I'd recommend a quote from the script of *Any Given Sunday*, a classic football film in which Al Pacino (Coach Tony D'Amato) imparts to his players: "You find out that life is just a game of inches. So is football. Because in either game, life or football, the margin of error is so small. I mean, one half step too late or too early, you don't quite make it. One half second too slow or too fast, and you don't catch it. The inches we need are all around us. They are in every break of the game, every minute, every second. When we add up all those inches that is what is going to make the difference between winning and losing, between living and dying*!*"

Finally, I'd highlight again that one most valuable personal quality, *charisma*—it's there for each of us to use, if we choose—that allows us to make it all happen. F. Scott Fitzgerald said of his character, Jay Gatsby, "He smiled understandingly—much more than understandingly. It was one of those rare smiles with a quality of eternal reassurance in it, that you may come across four or five times in a life. It faced—or seemed to face—the whole external world for an instant, and then concentrated on *you* with irresistible prejudice in your favor. It understood you just as you wanted to be understood, believed in you as you would like to believe in yourself, and assured you that it had precisely the impression of you that, at your best, you hoped to convey."

In leading you to win, Gatsby won as well. We *win,* truly, by our focus on others and by personally building a better world, one inch at a time.

Author Robin Sharma describes a man he'd met "who lived the philosophy I evangelize." Dr. Garth Alfred Taylor, born in Jamaica in 1944, was a gifted eye surgeon and humanitarian. For twenty-three years, he travelled to developing nations to selflessly help people regain their sight. His motto was "I came into this world with nothing and all I'm going to leave with is my conscience."

While aiding thousands of underprivileged individuals in the restoration of their sight after blindness, Dr. Taylor maintained, "Until I have no breath to breathe, I will continue to do this because I think I was chosen for this, not for money, not for compensation, but just to make the quality of life of my fellow human beings better."

We can be proud of our hard-earned accomplishments and successes—with the accompanying experiences, adventures, structures, and things that go along with *winning.* At the same time, we've been given a personal responsibility to respect, nurture, and touch others in the best positive way. Only then will our name, our impact, and the good we've done live *forever.*

May you be the *Who Wins* and your disciplined strategies the *Why* you've won!

APPENDIX A: Evaluating the win/loss aspects of two memorable sports events.

A Closer Look...Boxing's "Upset of the Century" and "The Worst Play Call In NFL History"

The specific process of moving toward or away from a win is better understood, I think, when one takes the time to observe and evaluate in detail any prominent national sports, political or business result. The day after a game, coaches spend hours with players reviewing game films to pinpoint and critique specific decisions and actions. Here are the "autopsies" of two notable sports events: one remarkable win and one shocking loss.

In Las Vegas, the odds were "42 to 1" against James "Buster" Douglas when he went up against Mike Tyson. Some casinos wouldn't even take a bet on the fight. The twenty-nine-year-old Douglas with 29 wins, 4 defeats, and 1 draw, with only 19 of his wins by knockout, wasn't thought to have a chance against the World Heavyweight Champion. The twenty-three-year-old "Iron Mike" Tyson had 37 wins, no defeats, and 33 of his wins were by knockout. For Tyson's 10th championship defense, a 12-round match on February 11, 1990 in Tokyo, Japan, Larry Merchant, of the HBO broadcast team predicted "...this fight is over before it begins or shortly thereafter."

Douglas's manager, John Johnson, explains in his 2007 book, *Tyson-Douglas: The Inside Story of the Upset of the Century,* that "The bout itself was being held in Tokyo because nobody in the United States had been willing to come up with big money to witness another non-competitive bout." Tyson's five previous heavyweight title fights had averaged fewer than three rounds. In his last title defense, he'd knocked out his opponent in ninety-three seconds.

James "Buster" Douglas shocked the boxing world by dominating the first nine rounds except for an eighth-round uppercut by Tyson that sent Douglas flat to the mat. He regained his composure by the referee's count of "nine," a second away from being counted out. The round ended a moment after Douglas stood up—the gift of thirty seconds to clear his head and regain his legs. After the fight, he commented that instead of letting Tyson's powerful punch take away his confidence, he viewed it simply as a "bump in the road—nothing less, nothing more."

In the next round, Douglas came out aggressively, anticipated and defended against Tyson's onslaught of punches, and again damaged Tyson with relentless jabs as he had in the earlier rounds. It seems that having just been knocked down, Douglas's immediate aggressive posture was unlike the careful, defensive position most other boxers would have made in that predicament. This seemed to surprise and confuse Tyson. At the beginning of the 10th round, Tyson did rock Douglas with a powerhouse right but it seemed to have no effect on the challenger's stamina.

With 1:52 left in the round, Douglas unloaded a

devastating uppercut to Tyson's jaw. With several sweeping blows to Tyson's head as he went down, Douglas finished the Champ and achieved the knockout that none of Tyson's thirty-nine opponents had come close to accomplishing. For that one night, James "Buster" Douglas was " Rocky" Balboa.

Later in the year, Douglas lost his first defense of his new championship to Evander Holyfield and was never a presence in the world of boxing again. He did, however, earn an unprecedented $25 million in that unsuccessful fight against Holyfield.

How did James "Buster" Douglas defeat "Iron" Mike Tyson in that historic upset in Tokyo?

Douglas did enter the World Heavyweight Championship fight with height and reach advantages— 6'4" with 83" reach—over Tyson—5'11" with 71" reach. However, his pro boxing successes had been inconsistent with some descriptions of him as a "journeyman" rather than a "contender." To earn the opportunity against world champion Tyson, Douglas had to defeat another mid-level contender, Oliver McCall. He won that July, 1989 fight with a ten-round decision but his performance was considered by his trainer as "lackluster."

Douglas did prepare well for the Tyson fight. His trainer, John Johnson, hired three sparring partners. They were "young, very tough...all about the same size as Tyson and taught to emulate the Champ's fighting style." Johnson relates, "They all arrived several months before the fight so that Douglas could work with fresh opponents every two or three rounds during the entire training period."

Before the Tyson fight, Douglas was financially broke, his wife had recently left him, and several weeks before the Tokyo fight, his mother passed away. Three days before the fight, Douglas got quite ill with a severe respiratory infection. Johnson thought they would have to cancel the title match. Douglas cut back his final training, and the Tokyo hotel's doctor provided medication that reduced Douglas's symptoms.

Douglas used the setbacks of his mother's death and his illness just days before the fight as motivators. With crystalline focus on victory, he relied on something his father, a successful boxer, had taught him: "When a guy is a strong thrower, especially a man over 200 pounds, keep working in the ring, don't get excited, and most important, stick to a game plan." With trainer Johnson's astute guidance, Douglas developed a mindful game plan based on "focus and power" and "sticking to the movements" that he knew had worked for him in the past.

Douglas's game plan was scripted from the opening bell: "I went out there to establish control of the fight. You know, getting off first, not hesitating to see what he was going to do, but to get my shots off first and take it from there. Never lose control." Douglas added his opinion that the best defense was a good offense, and, indeed, he threw and landed twice as many punches in the fight as Tyson did. Post-fight, Tyson admitted that he'd been tortured by Douglas's relentless jabs and the close infighting and that he'd been unable to see or anticipate the final punch that put him out.

The Douglas-Tyson match could have ended in the eighth round when a struggling Tyson landed the devastating punch that put Douglas on the mat. But Douglas told a commentator after the fight, "I'm conditioned to go twelve rounds; that's what I'm conditioned for. And that's why I was able to get up from the knockdown. You know, it was a good shot, and I give him all the respect for that. But when I got up, it was, like, well, it's time to go ahead and get him out of there."

Douglas knew that the fight was nearly over when he was floored by Tyson's punch. He took the referee's count nearly to the end before getting to his feet knowing he'd also get a needed 30-second break.

Douglas's dedication to training before the fight, his willingness to strictly follow his game plan, his awareness of how much time was left in the contest, and his dismissal of the fear that had overwhelmed all of Tyson's other opponents served him well. Douglas had briskly jogged into the ring before the start of the match, complete with bouncing tassels. A commentator noted, "Who has ever seen a fighter run to the ring to fight Tyson?" These were the actions of a winner.

With some background in boxing myself and reference to various post-fight commentaries, I'll add that Tyson made two obvious mistakes in the bout. Either could have changed the outcome. In the 8th round, upon putting Douglas on the canvas, Tyson was slow to retreat to a neutral corner. The count for Douglas, as the rules require, could not begin before he did so. Thus Douglas got a few extra seconds of precious recuperation time. With 33 wins

163

by knockout, Tyson should have remembered the rule.

In the 10th round, upon being knocked down by Douglas's powerful upper cut and head blows as he went down, a confused Tyson searched for his lost mouthpiece on the mat and just missed standing up before he was counted out. A veteran should have known better. Tyson hadn't taken Douglas seriously and had seen no need to even look at films of Douglas's earlier fights.

What are the lessons from Douglas's unpredicted victory? Preemptively, Douglas had been able to effectively control and move past the growing pre-fight fear of Tyson that had been shown by his earlier opponents. Douglas had prepared a clear game plan and he stayed with it even after Tyson stunned him in the 8th round.

And how is a nearly inevitable win *lost*?

February 1, 2015. The National Football League's Super Bowl 49 is played in Glendale, Arizona. It's the New England Patriots vs. the Seattle Seahawks. It's a close game with New England ahead by 4 points and little time remaining. Miraculously, Seattle receiver Jerraine Kearse accomplished a juggling "circus" catch for a 35-yard gain clear to New England's 10-yard line. Two quick plays brought the ball to the 1-yard line with three downs, twenty-six seconds, and one time-out remaining. Seattle's key running back, Marshawn Lynch, had led the NFL in rushing touchdowns for the past two seasons.

Against all conventional football strategy, Seattle head coach Pete Carroll and his offensive coordinator,

Darrell Bevell, called an unusual play. Conventional "wisdom" in football would have kept the ball on the ground in an initial running play to cover that one short yard into the end zone for the win. Seattle instead started with a pass into tight coverage, which was intercepted by New England's Malcolm Butler, undrafted rookie, for the first interception of his career. As the remaining seconds wound down, New England won the Super Bowl, 28-24.

CBS News called that fateful passing attempt "The Play That Will Live in Infamy for Seattle." Other commentators described it as "The Worst Play Call in NFL History." Coach Pete Carroll attempted to justify the call as an attempt to "manage the clock," that is, to reduce the seconds left for New England to regroup and score in the other end zone after Seattle got their needed TD. It's likely, too, that he hoped to catch New England off guard with an unexpected play. After all, they'd brought Seattle the 2014 Super Bowl championship a year earlier.

But what exactly did New England do to win with Seattle on the 1-yard line, ready to score? Malcolm Butler, who made the interception, told reporters after the game, "I remembered the formation they were in, two receivers stacked, I just knew they were going to a pick route. I just beat him (Seattle receiver Ricardo Lockette) to the route and just made the play." Butler recognized the play pattern from team practice and films of Seattle games, in New England's effort to anticipate the formations they'd be up against. They had three pass defenders in the end zone.

But was the pass really a terrible call? Sports

commentator Bill Branwell likely answered it best in his online column after the game. He agreed with coach Carroll that a quick touchdown with as many as twenty seconds left on the clock might have allowed new England a last ditch drive back for at least a tying field goal.

If Seattle had run on that critical second down and not gotten in, they'd have had to use their final time out as by then, with as few as ten seconds or so remaining, there may not have been enough time to run another play without it. A third down, then, couldn't have been a run as the clock could have run out. The situation wasn't quite as simple as it had first seemed to the fans and armchair quarterbacks!

What would have been the smart play strategy? Agile Seattle quarterback Russell Wilson could have burned off more seconds with the ball on that second down and then thrown out of the end zone—safe from interception. The third down, then, could have been a run by powerhouse Marshawn Lynch, with a timeout remaining if he didn't get in. And one more run could have gotten it done with little, if any, time left for a New England comeback.

Again, this detailed autopsy of how Seattle lost the Super Bowl has value only if practical lessons toward winning are the result. Without knowing exactly what coach Carroll was thinking on the play call, I still suspect that he was trapped by over-thinking. While coach of the University of California's football team in the 2006 Rose Bowl, he had been strongly criticized post-game for a late fourth-quarter play call that allowed his opponents to secure the win in this prestigious contest. A winner simply can't be haunted by the past.

APPENDIX B: My favorite *winning* thoughts.

From any change, even the most difficult and incomprehensible, something good will come.

You cannot *tell* anyone anything. You can only help people see for themselves.

Nothing has any power except the power you give it.

Every thought you think creates a psychosomatic or physiological response.

Fear is that little darkroom where negatives are developed.

You are writing your own career resume with each performance.

An anxious mind cannot exist in a relaxed body.

If what you know now was enough, you'd already be where you want to go.

Life isn't about *finding* yourself, it's about *creating* yourself.

Instead of "I'll try" or "I think I can," say "I *will*."

The lifeblood of successful living is owning your choices.

Keep things simple and live up to your commitments.

Be willing and able to be happy on your own.

What something *should* be is what isn't. You must deal with what *is*.

Great relationships have no *demands.* They have *desires.*

Release the need to always be *right.*

If life were a chess game, then time is your opponent. Make sure every move and moment count.

You don't get rich by how much time you use; you get paid for what you produce.

To yourself, you are what you think. To the outside world, you are what you *do.*

ABOUT THE AUTHOR

Stephen Weigert earned a Master of Science (M.S.) degree in the psychology field from the University of Wisconsin system. His career has spanned over four decades in his unique variety of positions as an award-winning rehabilitation counselor, psychotherapist, life coach, national/professional race driver, and television/film/stage actor.

He's advised and coached over 10,000 individuals including CEOs, physicians, attorneys, professional athletes, and entertainers. Stephen has "walked the talk" with seventeen years in motorsports, over three decades as a competitive runner, plus training with a pro boxer and learning to play equestrian polo.

Throughout his adult life, Stephen has been a passionate collector of high-performance and classic luxury automobiles.

He is semi-retired and lives in Palm Beach, Florida.

Visit Stephen's website: palmbeach7.com
e-mail: palmbeach7@gmail.com

Made in the USA
Columbia, SC
17 October 2018